THE REAL RULE OF FOUR

Joscelyn Godwin

disinformation

Parts of this book have been adapted from
the author's previous publications, as listed in the Bibliography.

Published by:
The Disinformation Company Ltd.
163 Third Avenue, Suite 108
New York, NY 10003
Tel.: +1.212.691.1605
Fax: +1.212.473.8096
www.disinfo.com

Library of Congress Control Number:2004112404

ISBN: 1-932857-08-7

Printed in USA

Distributed in USA and Canada by:
Consortium Book Sales and Distribution
1045 Westgate Drive, Suite 90
St Paul, MN 55114
Toll Free: +1.800.283.3572
Local: +1.651.221.9035
Fax: +1.651.221.0124
www.cbsd.com

Distributed in the United Kingdom and Eire by:
Turnaround Publisher Services Ltd.
Unit 3, Olympia Trading Estate
Coburg Road
London, N22 6TZ
Tel.: +44.(0)20.8829.3000
Fax: +44.(0)20.8881.5088
www.turnaround-uk.com

10 9 8 7 6 5 4 3 2 1

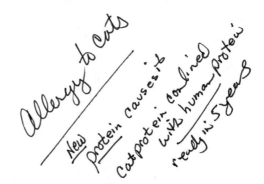

Allergy to cats

New protein causes it
Cat protein combined
with human protein
ready in 5 years

THE REAL
RULE OF FOUR

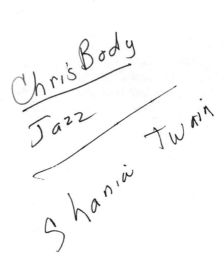

Chris Body

Jazz

Shania Twain

Table of Contents

Illustrations

Photographs and Map   64

Introduction

Readers of *The Rule of Four* are left with many questions. Is this 500-year old book with the unpronounceable name real, or have the authors just made it up? If it is real, does it contain the coded messages they say it does?

How about Francesco Colonna, the Roman nobleman? Was he a real character, and did he write the *Hypnerotomachia*? Did he die trying to save the treasures of the Renaissance from the bonfire of a mad monk? Where does history end and fiction begin?

What about all the other names that appear in *The Rule of Four*: writers, people from antiquity, titles of books, buildings, paintings, etc.—are they real? Should we assume that any educated person knows all about them? (The answer to that one is No, not even if they went to Princeton.)

What follows is not a treatise, but a guide-book. You can read a guide-book before you go on vacation, or take it with you, or read it afterwards to understand more about what you have seen. This book will serve all three purposes.

First, it gives you a vivid sense of the *Hypnerotomachia* (yes, it is a real book). It shows more of the illustrations and extracts from the text, so that you can see that it is like no other book on earth.

The Rule of Four is also a complicated book, put together from three different strands. This guide-book shows how they all work.

It explains the Princeton background, with a map of the campus and photographs of the places where the action of the novel takes place.

The characters in *The Rule of Four* have strong opinions about who wrote the *Hypnerotomachia*. So do other people, who know the work inside out. You will discover here that the author was not a nobleman at all, but a monk, which is all the stranger, since the *Hypnerotomachia* is erotic from beginning to end!

How about the secretive academy that tried to preserve the values of the Renaissance? There was such a one, and some people claim that it still exists. You can weigh the evidence here, and if you wish, go in search of it.

And what is the *Hypnerotomachia* really about? Who is Poliphilo, and his beloved Polia? Are they Romeo and Juliet, or historical celebrities in disguise? Is the whole thing a philosophical or psychological allegory?

As for all those learned references that the characters of *The Rule of Four* love to drop, every one of them is explained here, and there is a complete Index to the novel.

I have borrowed several portions of the present book from a longer work called *The Pagan Dream of the Renaissance.* The reader who is attracted by this order of ideas will find much more there, where the spirit of Poliphilo inspires a pagan make-believe world of gardens, grottoes, secret chambers, collections of rarities, courtly festivals, and even operas.

I would like to thank Andrew Nicholas Allfree and Rosalie Basten for their hospitality while I was writing this guidebook, and Principessa Emanuela Kretzulesco and Professore Maurizio Calvesi for the gifts of their own books, which I admire even when I cannot agree with their theses. Janet Godwin lovingly put up with the sacrifice of my summer.

Joscelyn Godwin
Hamilton, Oxford, Longueville-sur-Scie, Aups
Summer 2004

Chapter 1
The Real Hypnerotomachia

The object that goes under this resounding name (pronounced "HIP⁄ne⁄RO⁄to⁄MA⁄kia PO⁄li⁄FEE⁄li") is a book of 467 pages, a foot tall and broad to match, which was printed in the Serene Republic of Venice by the press of Aldus Manutius in the year of grace 1499. A few dozen copies are still scattered round the globe, most of them in the locked presses of libraries or behind the security systems of wealthy collectors. Quite a few probably lie in bank vaults, keeping company with silent Stradivarius violins, waiting to appreciate in value beyond the $320,000 that a fine copy of the book currently commands at auction.

How does the *Hypnerotomachia* come to be so much treasured? It is not enough that it is rare; many books are rarer still, but almost no one cares whether they own them or not. The main reason is that it is a most beautiful object, appealing to those who find beauty in books themselves, quite apart from the words and thoughts they contain. The beauty begins at skin⁄level, for the previous owner has usually gone to the expense of having the book bound in the hide of some domestic animal: a calf, a sheep, more rarely a pig, or, in the case of morocco leather, a goat. (The jacket of *The Rule of Four* shows a vellum [calf] binding, with raised bands highlighted in gold leaf.) One turns it over like a miniature treasure⁄chest, gloating at having the bibliophile's ultimate prize within one's hands—even if it belongs to a library. Whatever the title on the spine means, word-associations with hypnotism or erotica seem to promise mysteries and delights within.

Although Patrick Sullivan gave his son a framed reproduction of the *Hypnerotomachia's* title page, *(ROF, p. 82),* not much is given away there. Unlike later books of its size and pretensions, the title page boasts no symbolic engraving, no publisher's name, place, or date: just the bald statement:

THE HYPNEROTOMACHIA OF POLIPHILO, IN WHICH
IT IS SHOWN THAT ALL HUMAN THINGS
ARE BUT A DREAM, AND MANY
OTHER THINGS WORTHY
OF KNOWLEDGE AND
MEMORY.

* * *

* *

*

—to which some copies add a warning not to reprint the book within Venetian territory (as if they would, or could).

THE FINE ART OF TYPOGRAPHY

None but a very few readers pay any attention to the art of typography, but to a connoisseur, there is a pleasure to be had from simply contemplating a page of well-set type. He will notice how the precise form of each letter has been designed, so that they work shoulder-to-shoulder in any combination; how close together the lines are; the proportions of the margins. Whatever else the *Hypnerotomachia* may be, it is secure in its reputation as a typographic masterpiece. Its clear, round, legible type derives from the handwriting of ninth-century scribes under the empire of Charlemagne, whose manuscripts of classical works were rediscovered and prized in the Renaissance. The capital letters are based on the inscriptions carved on the monuments of Rome.

They are foursquare and sober, except for the palm⁄tree Y, and the Q with a tail as proud as a fox's brush. Each chapter begins with a summary of its contents set in these capitals, and a single much larger, decorative initial letter—those letters that conceal

POLIPHILO SEQVITA NARRANDO OLTRA TAN
TO CONVIVIO VNA ELEGANTISSIMA COREA CHE
FVE VNO GIOCO . ET COME LA REGINA AD DVE
PRAESTANTE PVERE SVE IL COMMISSE. LEQVALE
EL CONDVSERON ADMIRARE DELITIOSE ET MA-
GNE COSE, ET CONFABVLANDO EN VCLEAT AMEN
TE LA MAESTRORONO COMMITANTE DAL CVNE
DVBIETATE. FINALITER PER VENERON
AD LE TRE PORTE. ET COME ELLO
RIMANETE NELLA MEDIANA
PORTA, TRA LE AMORO-
SE NYMPHE.

ANTO EXCESSO ET INCOMPARABILE
gloria & triumphi, & inopinabile thesoro, & frugale de-
litie, & summe pompe, & solemne epulo, & lautissimo &
sumptuoso Symposio, di questa foelicissima & opulen-
tissima Regina recensito, si io distincta & perfinitamen
te la sua praecipua dignitate non hauesse condignamen
te expresso, Nó se mirauegli dicio la curiosa turbula, Imperoche qualunque di acuto ingegno & expedito, & di prodiga & fertilissima lingua orna
to & copioso ad questo enucleata, ne coadunatamente potrebbe satiffare.
Ma molto meno io che continuamente patiua per qualunque intima lá
tebra del mio inferuescente core, la indefinente pugna, quantúque absen
te di madona Polia, di omni mia uirtute occuparia & depopulabonda
praedatrice. De fora le molte miraueglie, di praecellentia inaudite di diuer
sitate, cose insuete & dissimile, inextimabile & non humane, Impero allu-
cinato & tutto aequalmente oppresso per omni mio senso, distracto per la
spectatissima uarietate la excessiua cótéplatióe, di púcto in púcto io nó
lo saperei perfectamente descriuere, ne dignaméte propalare . Chiunque
cogitare ualeria il richo habito & exquisito ornato, & curiosissimo culto
la perfecta & ambitiosa & falerata bellecia sencia alcuno defecto, La sum-
ma sapientia, la Aemiliana eloquentia, La munificentia piu che regia.
La praeclara dispositione di Architectura, & la obstinata Symmetria di
questo aedificio perfecta & absoluta, La nobilitate dellarte marmoraria.
La directione del columnamento, La perfectione di statue, Lornamen-
to di parieti, La uariatione di petre, Il uestibulo regale, amplissimo pe-
ristylio, Gli artificiosi pauimenti, Chi crederebbe di quanto luxo & im-

the author's name, which readers of *The Rule of Four* know all about. The typeface used in the *Hypnerotomachia* is one of the grandparents of all later roman typefaces, often receiving the homage of imitation. The typeface of the book you are reading is a modern recreation of it, called "Poliphilus," made by the Monotype Corporation in 1923.

Kelmscott Press, Doves Press, Nonesuch Press... the names of these private presses are so many tributes to the achievement of Aldus and his contemporaries. For half a millennium, the work of those Venetian craftsmen has been held up as an example of typography at its best. [Ill. 1, p.17] But the compositor of the *Hypnerotomachia*, however sound his instincts, faced an extra challenge, because he had to fit into his pages of text 172 illustrations of every shape and size. Some of the illustrations, in turn, contain lettering. This spurred Aldus Manutius's typographer to devise some ingenious solutions. On one page, he makes the block of type taper in a triangle, subtly balancing the upright triangle of the broken gravestone [Ill. 2, p.19]; in another, the text winds its way around two illustrations of military standards [Ill. 3, p.20, 21]. Whoever designed these pages was a playful genius in a recondite field.

ILLUSTRATIONS AND EROTICISM

Surprises were in store for the first owners of the *Hypnerotomachia* as they discovered, a few pages in, how richly it was illustrated. This was by no means usual practice in the incunabula period (that is, in books dating from the "cradle" [Latin *cunabula*] of printing, defined as up to and including the year 1500). Some early printed books were enhanced by hand-painted illustrations, or colored initial letters; the Gutenberg Bible left blank spaces for them. The *Hypnerotomachia* was one of the very first printed books to be illustrated throughout with black palmi q̄tro. Nelq̄le in una facie, dal frote dila fractuta era iscripto, & similmete oue era rupto p idicio di alcune litere pte fragmetate, & itegre, parte rimaste. Poscia nella subiecta corpuletia dalla circinante cinctura uerso el fondo, nellaquale erano appacte le anse, nel fronte dilla fractura era questa præstante scriptura.

HEVS INSPECTO
FACITO QVAE SOLACHRY
INFOELIX REGINA
AMENS AMANS
HOSPITIS PEREGRI
MEMISERAM ADM
INFAVSTO MVNER

N TO
PA
NOY
ΣΡΟΔΟΣ
ΡΑΛΛΙΑΝΕΙ ΠΑ
ΝΙΚΟΣ
ΤΡΑΤΟΣ
ΤΙΜΑΧΙΔΑ
ΤΙΝΝΙΑ

ΤΟΥΘΑΝΑΤΟΥ
ΒΕΒΑΙΟΤΕΡΟΝ ΟΥΔΕΝ

Relicti questi rupti monumenti, ad una destructa tribuna deueni nellaquale alquanto fragmento di museaco si comprendeua. Oue picto mirai uno homo affligente una damicella. Et uno naufragio. Et uno adolescetulo sopra il suo dorso equitante una fanciulla, nataua ad uno littore deserto. Et parte uedeuasi di uno leone. Et quegli dui in una nauicula remiganti. Il sequente distructo. Et ancora questa parte era in molti lochi lacerata, Non ualeua intendere totalmente la historia. Ma nel pariete crustato marmoreo, era intersepta una tabula ænea, cum maiuscule græcæ. Tale epigramma inscripto hauea. Ilquale nel proprio Idiomate in tata pietate me prouocaua legendo
si miserando caso, che di lachryme conte-
nirme non potui, dánando la rea for
tuna. Ilquale sæpicule perle
gendo, quanto io ho
potuto cusi il fe
ce latino.

and white woodcuts, and to make a virtue of this limitation. And what illustrations they are! I doubt that anyone has ever read it without first leafing through them all. Nor does one have to go very far to discover that there is something very odd about

Subfequéte & una attolleua uno tropheo cú
ṕcipua politura . In uno mucrone demigra
ua il fuṕmo haftile , fubdefcendédo uno co
ptorio fopra una rotunditate femifextante
craffa,i modo platineo refupinaua , nel me-
diano infculpta una formula circinata . Laquale uno pauculo di uafeo pediculo fuppri
meua.Pofcia una tabella cum tale fcriptura
maiufcula(QVIS EVADET ?)fubiaceua.
A quefta uno pomulo fubigeua ,& fubfequé
te unaltra rotun
datione,quale la
fuperna , ma mi
nore . Da uno a
lamento circú-
uallata & ad una
folida ouero ma
fficia fcutella fu
peraffidéte . Dal
laquale cótinua
to defcendeua u
no longiufculo
balufto , & po-
fcia una pileta.
    Similmente
portaua unaltra
nympha una ha
fta . Nellacumi-
nato era una figura ouola , cum orulo bul-
lato in circinao,& nel meditullo uno rotun
damento faphyreo la figura imitante di craf-
fitudine unciale,fubacta una affula,tale cum
titulo.NEMO.Et in medio di due ale,la ha
fta alquanto ballufticata intraiectaua . Infi-
mamente una fcutella fequiua,quale fopra e
recenfito.

Confequéte

this book. After a few innocuous pictures of woodland scenes,
architecture, etc., one encounters a group of dancers wearing their
heads backwards; inscriptions in unknown letters and picture-writing;
an elephant carrying an Egyptian obelisk on its back; a man pursued by

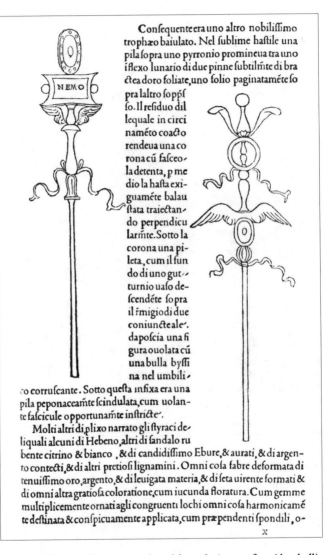

a winged dragon. Then comes the celebrated picture of an ithyphallic satyr approaching a sleeping woman. [Ill. 4, p.22] Whatever sort of story is this? A little further on, two charming young women are holding up a young boy who is preparing to piss, as if it were the most

ΠΑΝΤΩΝ ΤΟΚΑΔΙ

natural thing in the world. [Ill. 5, p.23] Which it is—but generally done without assistance.

The people in the pictures are almost all young women, evidently drawn to be attractive according to the canons of Renaissance art. There is one adult male, dressed in a beret and long gown, who appears in various combinations and relationships with them; what he is up to, one must read to find out. The classically educated reader (which meant anyone who got hold of the book before about 1950) recognizes some familiar scenes from

Graeco-Roman mythology, and the conventional figures of the gods: Jupiter, Venus, Cupid, Mars, etc. But are these scenes, well known from Ovid's *Metamorphoses*, events in the story? Does the story take place nowadays (i.e. circa 1500) or in classical times?

One comes next to the series of two-page spreads illustrating processions. [Ill. 6 a,b, p.24,25] These only serve to confuse the issue further. Are these Greek myths that the writer is recounting,

or are they events he witnesses himself? The processions all have a chariot or float, drawn by nothing as ordinary as horses, but by centaurs, elephants, unicorns, panthers, satyrs, and giant lizards. One of the floats (illustrated in the *The Rule of Four,* p. 65) carries a young woman who is apparently having sexual intercourse with a swan. (Classicists have no trouble with that: she's Leda, and the swan is really Zeus in disguise. Out of one of her eggs will hatch Helen of Troy.) The floats are all accompanied by a cheerful and jostling crowd, usually of nymphs in various stages of undress. One cannot help noticing that the artists have graced all the female nudes with that tiny line denoting the vulva, which has been conventionally omitted in fine art from that day to this.

I apologize for emphasizing the erotic element in the *Hypnerotomachia,* but you must put yourself in the position of someone looking through the book in past centuries, when sexual imagery did not leer from every newsstand. No such images had ever appeared in a printed book, and almost never in a manuscript,

either. The looker—not yet a reader—would have found this anatomical display deeply shocking; and after the shock, would either slam the book shut in disgust, or make sure that no one else was watching, and then continue. Later, some owners inked out the offending portions [Ill. 7, p.26]. For instance, in the Vatican Library copy, not only Leda and the Swan have been inked over, but a careful librarian has even erased "the leg of an elephant mistaken for the genital organ of his neighbor," as the architectural historian Liane Lefaivre remarks.

Censors have often emasculated the most famous and provocative illustration: the "Sacrifice to Priapus," which naturally appears, though reduced in size, in *The Rule of Four (ROF,* p. 64). The eye is magnetically drawn and held by the genitals at dead center, all the more astonished if not acquainted with the classical "herm": a human figure from the waist up, but a column or plinth from the waist down. In ancient Greece, herms were statues of the god Hermes, planted in the ground to mark the boundaries

of a town or region. It was an archaic and rustic custom—the earliest ones must have been quite crude, and of wood—and it seemed unnecessary to carve separate legs. However, the display of an erect phallus has an even more ancient history as a protective sign, warding off evil or warning enemies, symbolizing to a less prudish age the potency of the local divinity. So a proper herm (and one will find very few intact specimens in museums) has no hips or legs, but does have genitals. Here I show the version that was redrawn in the fashionable style of the 1540s for the French version of the *Hypnerotomachia*. [Ill. 8, p.27]

As we examine the picture more closely, we may well ask what the other people in the picture are up to. They are twenty-four in number, and beside two grumpy old men in the upper right-hand corner, they are mostly young women playing musical instruments, holding bottles, or tossing them up in the air. It is not all innocent fun and games: the three maidens in the foreground are twisting the tail of a donkey, cutting its throat, and catching its blood in a bowl. Apparently it is a pagan sacrifice, and the

ithyphallic idol is Priapus, the god of gardens and fecundity—but
is that all? Our imaginary sixteenth-century reader, even better
educated in the Bible than in the classics, might sense disconcerting

echoes. For instance, he might recall a passage in Chapter 5 of the Book of Revelation or Apocalypse: "four and twenty elders fell down before the Lamb, having every one of them harps, and golden vials full of odours"; and they all sang: "Worthy is the Lamb that was slain." The number of participants and their attributes correspond. The bottles look just like the "vials" in pictures of the Apocalypse, where the Elders are often equipped not just with harps, but with a whole orchestra of different instruments. Imagine the sixteenth-century reader, as likely as not a churchman, wondering whether the book he has in his hands is not only pornographic, but blasphemous.

Not a little horrified, but still fascinated, our imaginary reader leafs on through the book. From this point, things cool off somewhat, at least to the outward eye. There is a series of pictures of what seems to be a religious ceremony, with a robed and mitred celebrant and an acolyte—but unlike the rites of the Roman Catholic church, every participant here is a woman. Readers of

Dan Brown's *The Da Vinci Code* (and Martin Lunn's *Da Vinci Code Decoded*) do not need to be alerted to the possible significances of that! Further on in the book, there are a lot of tombstones with inscriptions, and various classical-looking objects like urns and standards. It is in this section that the typographer displays his most elegant combinations of word with image. In the last of the processions, which shows the Triumph of Cupid, the God of Love's entourage includes two satyrs carrying portable herms.

Lest we miss the details, a separate illustration highlights the anatomical correctness of these objects. [Ill. 9, p.28] A pair of well-endowed satyrs completes the presentation of the author's and artist's phallic obsessions. [Ill. 10, p.29]

Death and violence, even more than sex, are the obsessions that *The Rule of Four*'s Professor Taft displays with such gusto to his audience at the Good Friday lecture. In this trio of illustrations [Ills. 11, 12, 13, p.29, 30] Cupid, wielding a birch, is forcing two bound, naked women to draw his chariot. In the second picture, the merciless infant takes a sword and beheads the women, then

slices their bodies into pieces. Thirdly, a dragon, lion, eagle, and wolf feast on their flesh, while a clothed woman hides in the forest, watching, and Cupid flies triumphantly above the scene.

Does this really happen in the story? Strictly speaking, it does not. It is a dream, or rather a nightmare, related to her nurse by Polia, who is retelling it to an audience of nymphs. Polia in turn is a character in a longer dream related by Poliphilo. (This gives a hint of the complicated structure and the layers of unreality present in the *Hypnerotomachia*.)

The last part of the book has some pictures of normal people in church or temple interiors, and in houses. But abnormal

things are afoot here, too. In one of them, a woman is dragging a seemingly dead man along the floor by his feet. In another, she is embracing him upon her lap. [Ill. 14, p.31] In yet another, the couple is being pursued by angry women armed with sticks. Finally, there are some scenes that take place on the clouds, concluding with Cupid shooting his arrow into a disembodied female bust. The reader closes the book in a state of mind-bogglement.

AN INVENTED LANGUAGE

Having now looked through the book, which is sufficient to whet anyone's appetite, the time has come to read it. Here the trouble begins, for the *Hypnerotomachia*, though it passes as an Italian novel, is not written in the normal Italian of 1500, nor in the earlier language of Dante and Petrarch. The author has essentially tried to re-invent the Italian language by enriching its

vocabulary with hundreds of words adapted from Latin, and dozens from Greek. He has chosen Latin words so obscure that some of them only occur in a single Roman author. How anyone understood them in an age before proper dictionaries, I cannot imagine. All but the most learned scholars would just have had to skim over them. As if this is not enough to obstruct and deter most readers, the author writes in an extremely elaborate and wordy style, nominally Italian in grammar and syntax but more like the endless and scrambled sentences of Latin. Barely a noun lacks one or more adjectives, and more often than not these are in the superlative form. In short, the whole prose style is outrageously overdone, and on top of all that, it is in Venetian dialect.

Writers on the *Hypnerotomachia* often repeat the canard that its author used even more languages. Vincent Taft assures his audience that "it contains not only Latin and Italian, but also Greek, Hebrew, Arabic, Chaldean, and Egyptian hieroglyphics. The author wrote in several of them at once, sometimes interchangeably." *(ROF,* p. 118) A clever lawyer could defend this statement, but it is misleading, as is much of what Taft says (and that, no doubt, by design). I will take the claims one by one.

Hebrew appears in three places, all in illustrations, not in the text. While exploring the interior of the obelisk-carrying elephant, Poliphilo reads the inscriptions on a pair of statues, which appear in three languages: Hebrew, Greek, and Latin. (pp. 39, 40) The same three languages are shown above the three doors between which Poliphilo has to choose. [Ill. 15, p. 32]

Arabic appears in two places: above the three doors, just mentioned, and a few letters on a banner, along with Greek. [Ill. 16, p. 33] For more on these inscriptions, see p. 159.

Chaldean never appears, though Poliphilo speaks of other trilingual inscriptions (quoted below) as being in "Chaldean, Greek, and Latin." (p. 36) In any case, "Chaldean" is a misnomer. It is the name given by Renaissance scholars to the northern Semitic language that we know as Aramaic, the language probably spoken by Jesus of Nazareth (hence its revival in Mel Gibson's film.) Because some of the Jewish scriptures and commentaries were preserved in Aramaic versions, "Chaldean" counted as one of the sacred languages, and that is probably why it seemed suitable here.

Egyptian hieroglyphs: there are no authentic ones in the work, only made-up hieroglyphs based on the Greek writer Horapollo (who couldn't read the real ones, either) and on pseudo-hieroglyphic inscriptions from imperial Rome.

If one were to accurately reproduce the language and syntax of the *Hypnerotomachia* in English, one would have to invent some new words, and the result might come out like this sentence, in which Polia describes what happened in illustration 14:

> All on a sudden, O my most celebrated Nymphs, I felt as it were an amorous dulcitude, and with compasssionate and excessive alacrity my heart utterly dilacerated throughout its midst, whereby that blood that through dolor and overmuch fear had been constricted within itself, now in unfamiliar leticity I felt laxating the veins, and all undone and thunderstruck I was ignorant of what to say, if I did not with solvent audacity offer to his pallid lips as a little blandishment a lascivious and mustulent kiss, the two of us being gripped and constricted in amorous amplexity, like the intricately

convoluted serpents in the Hermetic Caduceus, and like the involuted verge of the sacrosanct Physician.

Even translated into acceptable English, the prose of the *Hypnerotomachia* pushes the limits, simply because of what the author has to say. Here is a more reader-friendly version of the above:

> Suddenly, O famous nymphs, I felt my heart ripped through the middle by a kind of amorous sweetness, pity and extreme joy—a sudden new feeling that caused the blood that had been blocked up by sorrow and excessive fear to course through my veins, overwhelming and astonishing me so that I did not know what to say. Instead, I took courage and offered to his still pale lips a lascivious and intoxicating kiss, then we joined and wound ourselves in amorous embraces like the intricately convoluted serpents around Hermes's caduceus, or the entwined rod of [Asclepius] the divine physician.

One could, of course, tell the story in more basic language still: "Listen, girls—I felt like the blood was all rushing to my heart and I couldn't say anything, so I just gave him a long kiss and we hugged each other real tight." That would match the typography of a pulp novel, but in the context it seems a little bald.

THE QUEST OF POLIPHILO

Assuming that the reader persists undeterred by the author's idiosyncratic style, he or she will discover that the *Hypnerotomachia* is divided into two parts, of which the first is very much the longer and more interesting. It tells the story in the first person of Poliphilo's search for Polia, the woman he has fallen in love with, and of their journey together to the Island of Cytherea, ruled by the goddess Venus. *Hypnerotomachia* is one of the author's invented words, made up from the Greek words for sleep (hypnos), love (eros), and combat or strife (machè). The title thus means *The Sleep-Love-Strife of Poliphilo,* or as the English translators prefer, *The Strife of Love in a Dream.*

Poliphilo's quest begins towards dawn, after he has spent a sleepless night agonizing over his unrequited love for Polia. He falls asleep and immediately wakens in a dense wood, like the one in which Dante began the adventure of his *Divine Comedy.* As he tries to find his way out of it, tearing his clothing on thorns and briars, he imagines the savage beasts that may be lurking there. He is tormented by thirst, and the moment he tries to slake it in a stream, phantom music draws him away. A wolf appears, but does him no harm. Instead, he finds himself facing a stupendous portal that spans an entire valley, from crag to crag. Poliphilo examines it and describes this first architectural wonder in minute detail, complete with measurements of the classically styled doorway. Above the portal is a giant mask of the Gorgon Medusa, and a stepped pyramid rises hundreds of feet. On top of the pyramid, there is an obelisk, and perched on this a statue of the goddess Fortuna (see description below). Poliphilo clambers up through the Medusa mask, and passes through the bowels of the mountains, where a winged dragon chases him through dark labyrinths. When all seems lost, he suddenly emerges into a pleasant land at the other side of the mountain, populated by the denizens of pagan legend. They are almost all female: nymphs and goddesses are now his companions, guides, and instructors. Although his inner turmoil is unassuaged, he is much cheered to find that this magical land is full of fascinating architecture. From now on, descriptions of the buildings, ruins, and other ancient remains takes up a large proportion of the text.

The nymphs who inhabit this land kindly take him under their care. First they bring him to a magnificent bath-house in which they proceed to bathe, and after some coaxing persuade him to join them. In scarcely veiled language, Poliphilo tells us how embarrassed he was because of being aroused by the sight of the naked nymphs. They find it hilarious and tease him mercilessly. At the bath-house, Poliphilo admires two sculpted fountains, already mentioned. One shows two nymphs holding up a child. It is a trick fountain, like the amusing waterworks in Renaissance gardens, for when Poliphilo steps on a certain flagstone, the child raises his member and pisses in his face. The nymphs again find his discomfiture immensely funny. The other fountain represents a sleeping nymph whose breasts dispense hot and cold water, and a satyr who is protecting her.

In view of the common interpretation put on this scene, I feel compelled to defend the satyr's reputation by reproducing the actual text. This will also show the difference between the plain but elegant illustrations of the *Hypnerotomachia* and the obsessively detailed descriptions.

> She held her lips slightly open so as to breathe, and the opening was carved and drilled out so that one could almost see her throat. Her loose tresses flowed over the cloth, with the finest hairs following the grooved or folded surface of the rumpled material. Her thighs were suitably fleshy, her plump knees slightly bent, showing her narrow feet which tempted one to reach out one's hand to stroke and tickle them; and the rest of her lovely body was enough to provoke even one made of stone, like herself. Behind her head was an arbutus tree with its evergreen foliage and many soft, round fruits, full of birds which seemed to be twittering and inducing the nymph's sweet slumber. At her feet there stood a satyr, all aroused in prurient lust: he had goat's legs, his lips adhered to his snub, caprine nose, and his beard divided at the chin into twin tufts of goatish curls. These also covered his flanks and his head, which

had hairy ears and a wreath of leaves, and seemed to be a mixture of goat and human. I reckoned that for this immensely skilled work, the sculptor must have been able to summon up nature's own creation in his mind.

This satyr had violently seized the arbutus tree by its branches in his left hand and was gallantly bending it over the sleeping nymph so as to make her a pleasant shade. With his other hand he held the end of a curtain that was knotted to the branches near the trunk. Between the leafy tree and the satyr there were two satyr-children, one holding a vase and the other with two serpents wrapped around its hands. *(HP,* pp. 71-72)

Poliphilo's humorous and amorous initiation continues with a visit to the ruler of this land, Queen Eleutherylida. She keeps a court staffed exclusively by ravishingly beautiful nymphs, and with them Poliphilo is treated to an eight-course banquet. There is no chatting allowed here, only musical accompaniment. The feasters are fed like baby birds by having food put into their mouths, and their mouths wiped with napkins: all this by the exquisite maids-in-waiting. At every course the tables are completely reset and decorated in different colors, and the attendant nymphs are dressed to match. Here is the description of one of the courses, which suggests that there may be a future for a *Poliphilo Cookbook:*

When this fourth rich course was removed, the table was relaid for the fifth with a crimson silk cloth, and the nymphs clothed in the same. The flowers were yellow, white, and amethystine Cairo roses; the food consisted of eight morsels of choicest, succulent roast pheasant meat, and as many pieces of a light white bread. The sauce was thus: fresh egg yokes with pine nuts, orange water, pomegranate juice, Colossine sugar and cinnamon. The dishes were of emerald, and so was the table of the sublime Queen.

Around the room are mosaics that depict the seven planets of traditional astrology: Moon, Mercury, Venus, Sun, Mars, Jupiter, and Saturn. There are also representations of the "children of the planets" or persons born under their influence. For example, lovers and musicians belong under Venus, traders and thieves under Mercury, paupers and cripples under Saturn. Although the queen's name Eleutherylida means free will, one gets the distinct feeling that everything in her court is rather rigid and regulated, presumably because there is no quarreling with the innate qualities bestowed by the planets at one's birth. After dinner there is a musical ballet that takes the form of a chess-game, with dancers as the chessmen. Of this entertainment Poliphilo says: "This solemn performance with its skirmishes, retreats and defenses lasted an hour. It involved rhythmical circulations, obeisances, pauses, modest restraints, and it filled me with such pleasure that I might well have thought myself transported to the heights of Olympus to taste a felicity I had never known before." (*HP,* p. 120)

Poliphilo leaves Eleutherylida's court sated with beauty and erotic stimulation, and is then faced with the choice of his future destiny. Two guides, Logistica (reason) and Thelemia (will, desire) lead him to the cliff face containing three doors, inscribed as we have seen in four languages (see ilustration 15). As each door opens, a group of women comes forth and they offer him the appropriate rewards. The leader of the first group is "an aged dame with a spinsterish air... She was in rags, squalid, skinny, poor, with downcast eyes... She dwelt at the entrance to a stony road... beneath a troubled, rainy sky and looming dark clouds." (*HP,* p. 136) This is how the author of the *Hypnerotomachia* presents the path to "Gloria Dei," the glory of God.

The second woman, wielding a golden sword, "had arms fit for Herculean labours... her soul was that of a ferocious giant," and she offers Poliphilo "Gloria Mundi," worldly glory. This holds some attraction to Poliphilo, but it is soon erased by

the opening of the third portal and the appearance of its mistress. "Her looks were wanton and capricious, and her joyful airs seized and captivated me with love at first sight of her." (*HP,* p. 138) Her portal leads to the Mother of Love. Helpless in the face of his own nature, and very much against the advice of Logistica, Poliphilo chooses this path.

After passing the portal, Poliphilo is met by a nymph who so much reminds him of Polia that he cannot help falling in love with her. Together they witness a series of "triumphs"— the processions already mentioned—that have as their theme the Loves of Zeus (the Roman Jupiter). There is Europa, carried away by Zeus in the form of a bull; Leda and the infamous swan; Danaë, whom the god impregnated in a shower of gold; and Semele, mother of Dionysus. Semele herself does not appear in her triumph, because, as the myth tells it, she asked her divine lover

to show himself in his true form, and the sight caused her to be vaporized. However, her son was rescued from her ashes and sewn up in the calf of Zeus's leg until his gestation was complete. Dionysus (the Roman Bacchus) became the god of wine and mysteries, and is represented on the float by his emblematic vine. [Ill. 17, p.40, 41]

The theme of these triumphs is that all beings, even Zeus as chief of the gods, is subject to Love. *Amor vincit omnia* (Love conquers all) is the repeated motto of the *Hypnerotomachia*, and appropriately underlined in *The Rule of Four*.

The next triumph is that of Vertumnus and Pomona, the god of gardening and the goddess of orchards, riding in a chariot drawn by satyrs. This leads to the rustic sacrifice to Priapus, the god of fertility. The bottles mentioned above are filled with milk, wine, and the blood of the sacrificed donkey, and the nymphs smash them at the base of his statue. (Imagine the mess!) Even in this richly detailed illustration, what is drawn is only a pale reflection of the author's purple prose.

The nymph next leads Poliphilo to the Temple of Venus Physizoa (Life-giver), where she confesses that she is indeed none other than Polia, his beloved. His rapture in finding her at last is equaled if not surpassed by what he feels on discovering this masterpiece of ancient architecture. He devotes twenty-three pages to describing the temple, in sufficient detail that it could

be constructed—and indeed, several later architects seem to have taken their inspiration from it. [Ills. 18, 19, p.42, 43] Here Poliphilo describes the inside of the dome.

> The huge dome displayed the greatest evidence of workmanship more nearly divine than human; but if it were human, it aroused astonishment that human ingenuity should make such an ambitious attempt in the founder's craft: for I judged that its great vastness had been made in a single solid fusion and casting of metal. I was astonished and overwhelmed by what I deemed to be impossible. Be that as it may, this bronze work consisted wholly of a vine sprouting from beautiful vases of the same material that were ranged perpendicularly above the columns. Thence they spread out branches, sprouts or shoots, and tendrils of dizzying intricacy, perfectly fitting the convex curve of the dome and all of the appropriate thickness. There were leaves, bunches of grapes, infants climbing and plucking them, flying birds, lizards and snakes, all modeled exactly from nature; and in between it was all transparent. [...] Everything was brightly gilded with pure gold, while the openings or interstices between the leaves, fruits, and animals appeared to be conveniently covered by crystalline plaques of various colors, like transparent gems. (*HP,* p. 201)

The temple is ten-sided, with an ambulatory all around it, separated from the central circle by columns. Between two of these is a doorway into an adjoining chapel, also circular, which is the site of the miraculous ritual in which Poliphilo and Polia are married. The High Priestess enters with a cortege of female acolytes and conducts an elaborate service, accompanied by signs and wonders. It includes the sacrifice of two swans and pair of doves, the pouring of libations of sea-water, the opening of a mysterious well, and the instant growth and blossoming of a fruit tree. The details of the ritual are a blend of ancient Roman rituals and marriage-rites, and near-quotations from the Catholic liturgy. When Poliphilo and Polia eat the fruit from the miraculous tree, the imagery blends the Christian Eucharist (Holy Communion) with memories of Adam and Eve eating the fruit in the Garden of Eden.

After this pagan wedding, the lovers go alone to the seashore to await the coming of Cupid and his boat, which is to ferry them to the Island of Cytherea, Venus' own realm. Although Poliphilo is now apparently married to Polia, he is still tormented by uncertainty and frustration connected with her, and raging desire aroused not only by his beloved but by the irresistible nymphs who have constantly attended him. Now that he is alone with Polia, uncontrollable lust fills his imagination with images of rape. Polia wisely arouses his other passion—the love of Antiquity—and sends him to examine the classical grave monuments and broken ruins of temples. Scrambling through undergrowth and marble-strewn ground, Poliphilo finds one example after another of elegant decoration, bas-reliefs, and lettering. The inscriptions in Latin, and less frequently in Greek, all tell of the misfortunes of lovers, spurned by each other or driven together to a premature end. He becomes so enwrapped in his antiquarian studies that he quite forgets about Polia. Suddenly he remembers her, and his mind fills with horrible imaginations of what may have happened to her. But when he rushes back, panic-stricken, he finds her where he left her, sitting serenely by the shore.

In due course Cupid arrives in the form of a naked child, with gold-dusted, peacock-feathered wings. His boat is rowed by six more exquisite nymphs whose names translate as Extravagance, Youth, Luxury, Happiness, Safety, and Belonging to Venus. Cupid helps the little boat onward by spreading his wings to act as sails. On the mast is hoisted a banner bearing the motto *Amor vincit omnia*. Colonna's Cupid may be a child, but he is extremely knowing and, for all his immaturity, already has a history of subjection to his own powers. As legend tells, he wounded himself with his own arrow, and fell in love with Psyche, whom he visited incognito for nocturnal lovemaking. (The tale of Cupid and Psyche is told in Apuleius's picaresque novel, *The Golden Ass, or The Metamorphoses,* which was one of the main influences on the *Hypnerotomachia.*) Here Poliphilo tries to find words equal to the vision of the god of love, which surpasses mortal sight:

> I would have made every effort to keep my eyes reverently and modestly fixed on the divine pilot; and although my feeble sight could not easily support so incommensurate an object, by half-closing my eyelids I was able to see something of the divine boy of many shapes. Sometimes he appeared to me in a double form, sometimes triple, and again at other times he showed himself in countless images. Together with Polia, he made our journey fortunate, blessed and glorious. And on the way, amorous Cupid in the prow spread out the sacred feathers of his wings, between which Canens, the lover of Pico, sported. They flashed brighter than refined gold with various cheerful colors, making a turning circle on the waves that was even more beautiful and charming than Euclid's triangular prisms of crystal, when brought close to the eye. *(HP,* p. 285)

Not only the eye, but the ear is brought to the pinnacle of ecstasy on this voyage. Poliphilo next describes the singing of the nymphs as they celebrate the universal power of love. Those familiar with Renaissance music will find a special pleasure in this description; but there is something universal about it that transcends time and place.

Now the sailor-nymphs began to sing, with sweetest notes and heavenly intonation quite different from human ones, and with a vocal skill beyond belief, a lovely concert with harmonized voices and bird-like melody. I felt that I would expire from excessive sweetness, because my beating and wounded heart was so stirred from its place by the beauty that it seemed to be escaping from my lips. The nymphs continued, fluttering their tongues against their sonorous palates and dividing and trilling even the shortest flagged notes into two or three. First they sang in pairs, then in threes, then in four parts and lastly in all six, their tremulous, rosy little lips opening moderately and closing neatly. They performed the well-modulated airs in musical rhythm, with a voice that was honey to the hot and swooning heart and its tiring postponement of love; and sometimes their voices sighed and gently sobbed, so as to make one forget and neglect one's natural desires. They sang to stringed instruments, celebrating the benefits and qualities of love, the merry affairs of great Jupiter, the soothing heart of holy Erothea, the lascivity of festive Bacchus, the fecundity of nurturing, yellow Ceres, the dainty fruits of Hymen, performing them rhythmically in poetic modes and metrical melodies. (*HP*, p. 285)

IN THE REALM OF VENUS

Venus's realm is a circular garden-island, enclosed with a thick hedge. It is laid out in concentric circles that blend nature with art, plants of every description with architecture made from rare marbles and precious stones. Cupid progresses through its regions blindfolded (for "love is blind"), enthroned on a two-wheeled chariot drawn by two giant lizards. Poliphilo and Polia follow it on foot, tied together like captives at a Roman general's triumph—but tied with "flowery garlands and rosy withies."

[Ill. 20 a, b, p.48, 49] As they traverse the island, we read of the many different types of gardens with their trees and plants, all named with encyclopedic thoroughness. A particular specialty of Venus's gardeners (who of course are never seen at work) is topiary, the art of clipping hedges of yew and box into shapes. This seems to be the feature of the garden in which nature and art most closely coincide. There are also geometric and symbolic knot-gardens, and a variety of complicated fountains.

The climax of the novel is set in a circular theater that occupies the center of the island, with an audience of dancing and singing nymphs. In the middle of the theater is the Bath of Venus herself, where Poliphilo and Polia have an epiphany of the goddess in her nudity. Venus turns to Polia and speaks with unmistakable echoes of Catholic prayers and benedictions:

> Pretty Polia, my devotee, your holy libations, your devoted
> services and your religious ministrations have propitiated

me and made you worthy of my sweet and fruitful graces. Your sincere supplications, inviolate sacrifices and solemn ceremonies have pleased me, and your devoted heart and observances as a novice incline me with beneficence, favor, munificent liberality and protection toward you. I also wish that your inseparable companion Poliphilo, who is here burning with love for you, be numbered equally among the true and happy lovers. After being cleansed of every plebeian and vulgar stain, and from all unclean impiety into which he may have fallen, he shall be suffused with my dew and purified, and shall give himself in perpetual dedication to you. He shall be ready and willing to please you, and shall refuse you nothing that you desire. And both of you, loving each other equally, shall serve my amorous fires with full consent and everlasting increase, and enjoy blessed and glorious bliss under my safe protection for the rest of your lives. (*HP*, pp. 364-365)

Then the god Mars arrives, strips off his armor, and enters the bath with the goddess, whereupon the company discreetly withdraws. Poliphilo and Polia settle down with their attendants in an enclosed garden. This houses the fountain and tomb of Adonis, the mortal beloved of Venus who, against her wishes, went off hunting and was killed by a boar. After contemplating this sad memorial, the assembled nymphs persuade Polia to tell them her own story. Thus the first book of the *Hypnerotomachia* ends.

ARCHITECTURAL OBSESSIONS

What makes Poliphilo's dream so vivid, and so important as a witness to the obsessions of its time, is the fact that hero and author are repeatedly distracted from their love-quest by the monuments that they encounter. Even before Poliphilo meets the dragon, he has spent several pages describing three gigantic statues: a bronze horse which a crowd of infants is trying to ride, a recumbent colossus of metal, and the hollow elephant carved from a single block of obsidian (black volcanic glass) with an obelisk on its back. Here is part of Poliphilo's description of the colossus, which shows the author's visual imagination, his inventive ingenuity, and, at the end, his contempt for the lesser achievements of his own age. He must have been writing this at the very time when Michelangelo and Leonardo da Vinci were making their surreptitious dissections of corpses, the better to depict human anatomy in their art.

> This colossus lay on its back, cast from metal with miraculous skill; it was of a middle-aged man, who held his head somewhat raised on a pillow. He seemed to be ill, with indications of sighing and groaning about his open mouth, and his length was sixty paces [300 feet]. With the aid of his hair one could climb upon his chest, then reach his lamenting mouth by way of the dense, twisted

hairs of his beard. This opening was completely empty; and so, urged on by curiosity, I proceeded without further consideration down the stairs that were in his throat, thence into his stomach, and so by intricate passageways, and in some terror, to all the other parts of his internal viscera. Then oh! what a marvellous idea! I could see all the parts from the inside, as if in a transparent human body. Moreover, I saw that every part was inscribed with its proper name in three languages, Chaldaean, Greek and Latin. Everything was there that is found inside the natural body: nerves, bones, veins, muscles and flesh, together with every sort of disease, its cause, cure and remedy. All the closely-packed organs had little entrances giving easy access, and were illuminated by small tunnels distributed in suitable places around the body. No part was inferior to its natural model. And when I came to the heart, I could read about how sighs are generated from love, and could see the place where love gravely hurts it. All this moved me deeply, so that I uttered a loud sigh from the bottom of my heart invoking Polia—and instantly heard the whole machine resonating, to my considerable fright. What an object it was, surpassing the finest invention, as even a man ignorant of anatomy could appreciate! O mighty geniuses of the past! O truly golden age, when Virtue went hand in hand with Fortune! But you have bequeathed to our own age only Ignorance, and its rival Avarice. (pp. 36-37)

Poliphilo's awe before the three great statues is nothing in comparison to his reaction at the pyramid-portal. Like the modern visitor to certain unexplained and oversized relics of ancient ingenuity—the plinth of the Temple of Jupiter at Baalbek, for example, with its 600-ton blocks, the Tomb of Theodoric at Ravenna, with its 300-ton monolithic domed roof built by "barbarians" on the eve of the Dark Ages, or the Pyramids of Giza—Poliphilo wonders how on earth they were made. Here is his description of the statue that tops the structure. It represents the goddess Fortuna, who is slippery and changeable and must be seized by the forelock if one is to gain her favor.

> A firm base of orichalcum was placed with care and artistry upon the very top of the obelisk, and above this a revolving machine or cupola was fixed on a stable pin or spike. It held a statue of a nymph, elegantly made of the same material and such as to astound anyone who looked at it long and carefully, proportioned so that when one looked up at it in the air, it appeared to be of perfectly natural size. Over and above the size of this statue, it was astonishing to consider the temerity with which such an object had been raised so high, indeed into the air. Its garments were blowing, revealing part of its plump calves, and two open wings attached between its shoulders showed that it was flying. Its beautiful face was turned towards the wings with a kindly expression, and its tresses floated loosely above its forehead in the direction of its flight, while the crown or cranium was bare and almost hairless. In its right hand it held the object at which it was looking: an elaborate cornucopia filled with good things, but turned towards the earth; and it held its other hand tightly over its bare breast. This statue revolved easily at every breath of wind, making such a noise, from the friction of the hollow metal device, as was never heard from the Roman treasury. And where the image's feet scraped against the pedestal beneath them, it made a jingling unmatched by the tintinnabulum in the great Baths of Hadrian, nor by that of the five Pyramids standing in a square. This tall obelisk left me in no doubt that there was none other resembling or comparable to it,

not even that of the Vatican, nor the Alexandrian, nor the Babylonian. It contained such a host of marvels in itself that I stood stupefied by the thought of them. Above all there was the immensity of the undertaking, and the exceeding subtlety, the extravagant and acute ingenuity, the great care and exquisite diligence of the architect. What bold invention of art, what power and human energy, what organization and incredible expense were needed to hoist this weight so high into the air, to rival the heavens? What capstans and pulley blocks, what cranes, compound pulleys, frameworks of beams and other lifting machines? It was enough to silence every other structure, however large or incredible. (*HP*, pp. 23-24)

The reader will have noticed Poliphilo's disconcerting habit of dropping the names of ancient authors and buildings as though expecting one to know exactly what he is referring to. I might add that the characters of *The Rule of Four*, in a more modest way, have borrowed this feature of the Poliphilic style. That is the reason for Chapter 6 of the present book, in which all their references are explained.

In connection with this architectural obsession, *The Rule of Four* contains the surprising statement that Poliphilo "admits to having sex with buildings. At least once, he claims the pleasure was mutual." (*ROF*, p. 63) This is based on a passage in Liane Lefaivre's book on the *Hypnerotomachia*, where she writes that "In three cases, Poliphilo manages to locate the appropriate orifice through which he can engage in sexual congress with particular buildings. His response, always described at length and in much detail, is sheer coital ecstasy. In one instance the effect on the building is mutual." (Lefaivre p. 66) I see no reason to accept this kind of Freudian interpretation. Certainly the author of the *Hypnerotomachia*, or his mouthpiece Poliphilo, is plunged into an ecstasy by the contemplation and examination of ancient buildings. But to call this "sexual congress" is to mistake the nature of Eros, the god of desire. The erotic includes the sexual, not the other way round.

There is plenty of the normal kind of eroticism in the *Hypnerotomachia*, as Poliphilo responds to the feminine figures that populate his dream. We have seen in his description of the anatomical colossus how intensely he imagines every detail. Here he describes, with equal attention to the particular, the nymphs who row Cupid's boat:

> This admirable and extraordinary vessel was expertly rowed by six very capable and masterful girls. The oars, including their blades, were of shining snowy ivory, not like a white radish but naturally glossy. The rowlocks were of gold, and the ties of many-colored twisted silk. These maidens were luxuriantly dressed in transparent material that waved and wafted in the brisk and gentle breezes. Girdled against the wind, it danced and revealed with voluptuous ostentation that the members to which it clung were in the flower of their youth. Some had their heads adorned with a tangle of abundant, pale blond hair, while others bore copious glossy locks blacker than Indian ebony. How lovely it was to see the contrast of these two extremes! The flesh of their faces, shoulders and breasts was perfectly white, and generously encircled with their black hair arranged in curls and tresses and lasciviously bound with silver threads, knotted and netted so as to be more pleasant and grateful to the senses than any voluptuous vision, and apt to draw one away from any other sight. They wore massed orient pearls around their necks, surpassing the one that Julius bought for his dear Servilia. Some also had attractive wreaths of roses

and other flowers wound into the curly hair whose ringlets shaded their bright foreheads. Around their straight and milk-white throats they wore sumptuous necklaces of conical gemstones in various matching colors. Moreover, they were tightly belted crosswise close below their firm little breasts, which presented an obstinate obstacle to their blouses; for although imprisoned, at the slightest nudge they returned briskly to their places. (*HP*, p. 276)

Perhaps the most striking aspect of Poliphilo's dream world is the actual appearance in it of the gods and goddesses of classical antiquity, notably Cupid and his mother Venus as indispensable actors in the drama. At Venus's Fountain, where the goddess meets her lover Mars, there are two other divinities in attendance, Ceres, the goddess of "cereals" and agriculture, and Bacchus. A well-known Latin tag states: "Without Ceres and Bacchus, Venus grows cold," i.e., one cannot feel amorous without first satisfying the stomach with bread and wine. The author grouped these divinities together, anticipating (and maybe inspiring) one of the favorite painterly themes of the Mannerist era. Since the book was never put on the Index of Prohibited Books by the censors of the Roman Catholic Church, it must have been assumed that all this paganism was merely allegorical and harmless to the faith. But the author's enthusiasm for every feature of the pagan world and the sustained atmosphere of eroticism, obsession, and ecstasy make it very hard to believe that he was really talking about something else.

POLIA'S STORY

The second book of the *Hypnerotomachia* is mostly narrated by Polia, for the entertainment of the nymphs. Poliphilo is present, but he does not speak: instead, Polia relates for page after page his conversations with her and the letters that he wrote her during the time of his unsuccessful wooing. She tells in much detail of her noble Roman ancestors and her family's history in the north Italian city of Treviso. There, she says, she reached the flower of her age in the year 1462. With this mention of a contemporary date, we enter a different world and a different mood from Poliphilo's dream—although, strictly speaking, the Polia who speaks is only a dream figure, and consequently all she says could be merely his fantasy. The style of Book Two is entirely different from the hyperbolic descriptions of Book One, sometimes resembling the popular, ribald tales of Boccaccio, and sometimes seeming like a mere exercise in rhetoric. It was almost certainly written earlier, and then incorporated into the epic scheme.

Polia tells how she fell ill of the plague, but promised the chaste moon-goddess Diana that if she recovered, she would dedicate her life to service in Diana's temple. She did so, and duly entered on a life of chastity. But Poliphilo had caught a glimpse of her and fallen in love at first sight. With much difficulty he tracked her down, watched, then approached her when she was praying alone in the temple, and declared his love. Polia, true to her vows, was deaf to his pleas. She sent him away, ignored his letters, and, when he returned, treated him with such cold disdain that he collapsed lifeless before her. Polia dragged away his body by the feet and hid it in a corner of the temple.

Nothing about this would have been discordant with a contemporary situation. Diana's temple, both as described and as pictured, is a scarcely-disguised Italian convent, and Polia is a novice nun. This kind of drama must have played itself out many times in Catholic Europe.

Having, as it were, died, Poliphilo's soul now ascended to the realm of the gods, and besought Venus, through the mediation of her son Cupid, to have mercy on him and make Polia love him. The goddess consented; the image or soul of Polia was brought forth, and Cupid shot an arrow into its breast. Poliphilo's soul was permitted to return to its body. This was the very moment of Polia's change of heart, which I have given in three versions above, and her voluntary kiss and embrace of her lover.

But before that revelatory moment, Polia had spent a very disagreeable night. She had had appalling nightmares of Cupid dismembering naked women and feeding their limbs to beasts (the episode so beloved of Professor Taft), and of two ruffians who broke in and were about to rape her. Lest it be thought that the author's powers of description are restricted to a besotted aestheticism, here is the description of this episode.

> My shaken body relaxed in its first sleep, which is the best, sweetest and most refreshing; it stretched out and slept in the silent night. But it was as if I had the eumeces stone at my head: I seemed to hear a great noise as though bolts were being shot, locks forced, and burglars breaking the iron bars and violently throwing open the doors on the threshold of my bedroom. Then there entered heedlessly, with rapid and hurrying steps, two horrible executioners with bulging and swollen cheeks, coarse clothing, and gross and shocking peasant gestures. They looked wild and angry, with fearful eyes that were more piercing than those of the deadly basilisk: large and round, they rolled in their cavernous sockets beneath bushy eyebrows, dense and bristly with long thick hairs like those of the Sileni. They had huge mouths with pendulous lips, thick, swollen and curling, the color of putrefaction; the great teeth in their jaws were uneven, rotten and rusty like old iron, destitute of gums and abandoned by the lips, which left them uncovered. They stuck out of their gaping mouths like a boar's tusks, foaming in the chase, and gave off a foul stink. Their faces were hideous and deformed, dusky and leaden in color, covered in fissures and wrinkles.

Their goat-like hair was greasy and filthy, grizzled with black and gray: it looked like the bark of an old elm-tree. Their broad, calloused hands were bloody and slimy, with stinking fingers and vile nails that they seemed eager to use cruelly against me, a poor maiden. They swore and blasphemed, furrowing their hairy brows and lowering their eyelids above their turgid cheeks. They wore two twisted cords stretched over their muscled shoulders, and hatchets—the lictors' instruments—were stuck in their belts. Their naked bodies were clothed in goatskin, which I suspected to be the costume of bloodthirsty torturers and the most polluted of men. I heard them bellow with ghastly and terrible voices, like a bull roaring in a hollow cave, as with insolent arrogance and presumption they abused me, saying: "Come on now, you proud and wicked one! Come, come, you rebel, you enemy who opposes the rule of the immortals! Come, come, you silly girl who despises and ignores her own pleasure! You rascal! You rascal! Now you're going to get the divine revenge you deserve, you guilty woman: yesterday you saw two other young criminals just like you torn limb from limb, and in a moment the same will happen to you!" (*HP*, pp. 405-406)

Polia's kindly nurse interprets the nightmares as warnings about refusing the duties of love, and tells her a cautionary tale about another young woman who had done this, and ended up married to an impotent old man and killing herself. Properly scared, Polia returns to the Temple of Diana, drags Poliphilo's body out of hiding, and tries to revive it. Little does she know that this is the very moment at which Cupid in heaven has wounded her soul, and Venus has sent Poliphilo's soul back to earth. Consequently he comes back to life in her arms, and she falls instantly in love with him. Her virgin sisters angrily drive the couple out of Diana's temple, and they take refuge in the Temple of Venus, where the priestess is only too happy to hear their story and to approve their union.

That is the end of Polia's story. The nymphs thank her and disperse, leaving her and Poliphilo alone by the Fountain of Adonis.

> Then, winding her immaculate, milk-white arms in an embrace around my neck, she kissed me, gently nibbling me with her coral mouth. And I quickly responded to her swelling tongue, tasting a sugary moisture that brought me to death's door; and I was straightway enveloped in extreme tenderness, and kissed her with a bite sweet as honey. She, more aroused, encircled me like a garland, and as she squeezed me in her amorous embrace, I saw a roseate blush strongly suffusing her naturally snowy cheeks; while on her stretched skin, a mixture of scarlet rose with the calm glow of ivory was shining with the utmost grace and beauty. The extreme pleasure caused tears like transparent crystal to form in her bright eyes, or like pearls finer and rounder than Euriale's or than those that Aurora distils as morning dew upon the roses. This deified, celestial image then dissolved in the air, like the smoke, perfumed with musk and ambergris, that rises to the ether from a stick of incense, to the great delight of the heavenly spirits as they smell the strangely fragrant fumes. Quickly she vanished from my sight, together with my alluring dream, and in her rapid flight she said, "Poliphilo, my dear lover, farewell!"

NOTHING BUT A DREAM?

"Oh, I've had such a curious dream," says Alice after her adventures in Wonderland. Poliphilo's story, like hers, begins and ends in the real world, but to judge from his desperate mood at the beginning and desolation at the end, he never was the lover of a woman called Polia. There is no evidence that she ever existed outside his dream. The whole novel resembles those Irish stories of people who wandered into Fairyland, lived there for years, married a fairy husband or wife, had children, grew old… then woke up the next day.

But after 467 pages, can one really say that none of it happened? Such an epic work of the creative imagination cannot be so easily dismissed. Alice and her adventures in Wonderland and through the Looking Glass are more real to many children than the drabber realities of life at home and school. While the stories of the Bible or the Koran may be nothing but imaginary inventions, to some people they are real enough to live and die for. Whoever we are and whatever we believe, more of our life is lived in the imagination than most people like to admit. Our day-to-day existence is crammed with dreams, fantasies, and long excursions into the past, in the form of stories we tell to others and to ourselves. Just like Poliphilo, we chew over past experience and try to make sense of it, or imagine how it might have been. The books we read become part and parcel of that experience. Reading them is a parenthesis within our world, a story within our story, and a dream within our dream. For as the author proclaims, "all human things are but a dream."

But enough of such thoughts! We do not wish to end up like the "book-learned people" described in *The Rule of Four*, who are convinced that "life as we know it is an imperfect vision of reality, and only art, like a pair of reading glasses, can correct it." (*ROF*, p. 44)

Chapter 2
The Three Layers of The Rule of Four

Like the *Hypnerotomachia*, *The Rule of Four* is constructed on several levels that differ in time-scale and in narrative style. One level concerns the events of two days in 1999. The second level, or layer, wraps around the first one, describing events both before and afterwards. The third level is a story of things that happened five centuries before.

LAYER I. PRINCETON UNIVERSITY, APRIL 2-3, 1999.

The action of *The Rule of Four* opens at about 7:00 p.m. on April 2, 1999, (*ROF,* p. 5) and closes at about midnight on Saturday, April 3. The authors were no doubt aware of the rules of ancient Greek drama, which dictated that the action of a play should take place within a single day, and in a single location. These are known in literary theory as the "unity of time" and the "unity of place." Although the novel stretches its "day" to about 30 hours, and extends its place all over the Princeton University campus, this layer pays heed to the two classical unities.

The parts of the novel that tell this story are easily distinguishable, for they are all in the present tense. Here is a summary of the main episodes, tracking the movements of Tom Sullivan around the Princeton campus:

ROF page

17	enters the tunnels near Dillon Gym shortly after 7:07 p.m.
25	inside the tunnels; it is 7:24 p.m.
27	it is 7:29 p.m.
32	emerges from the tunnel system near Rockefeller College
33	into Holder Hall and Katie Marchand's room
36	leaves Katie's room, heading for Firestone Library
53	into library; Paul receives diary from Stein
58	leaves library
73	to art museum; trustees' meeting. Due to meet Curry at 8:30 p.m. (p. 11)
80	back to Dod Hall (dormitory of the Four), finding room ransacked
87	drives to Ivy Club with Gil; eats dinner there
105	to lecture hall for Taft's lecture
125	in courtyard beside the chapel; Stein falls from window
137	drives to parking lot beyond Dod
159	back to dormitory, watches television
166	enters art museum with Paul; is there at 11:54 p.m. (p. 216)
183	to Woolworth music building; is there at 12:30 a.m. (p. 218)
191	back to dormitory and to sleep

Saturday, April 3, 1999

215	wakes at 9:30 a.m.
216	to darkroom at the *Prince* office
243-44	back to dormitory; finds note left by Paul
246	leaves at 10:25 a.m. with Charlie; meets Paul, walks to McCosh Hall

While the characters are of course fictional, the Princeton setting is authentic, and all the buildings mentioned do exist. Most of them are ordinary departmental or university buildings, but the eating clubs are an institution peculiar to Princeton. In *The Rule of Four* we read of four of them: Ivy Club, Cloister Inn, Cottage Club, and Tiger Inn. Their history began after the ban on Greek-letter fraternities, enforced by President Maclean in 1855. This drove students to seek other venues for dining and social life, and a large number of informal clubs grew out of this need. The first such club to obtain university recognition was the Ivy Club in 1879, and many other clubs appeared (and disappeared) over the next hundred years.

As with the fraternities of other universities, there has always been tension around Princeton's eating clubs. Opponents maintain that they perpetuate elitism and cliquism. Defenders point out that they fill a social void and lay a basis for lifelong friendships. Their presentation in *The Rule of Four* is ambiguous. The venerable Ivy Club, which figures most prominently in the novel, gets a favorable press, especially for having accepted Paul Harris as a member: a young man socially inept and at the bottom of the economic ladder. The Tiger Inn, on the other hand, is responsible for the gross and blasphemous display following the

Good Friday lecture (*ROF,* pp. 131-133). Only insiders can detect the innuendos and subtle gibes that no doubt lurk between the lines.

It is important to realize that *The Rule of Four* is a novel of *undergraduate* life, and that no great university exists for its undergraduates alone, or even primarily for them. There are adults there, too, as graduate students and faculty, who have better things to do with their leisure than play paint-ball in tunnels. Unfortunately, the only representatives of these strata in the novel are Stein, for the graduate students, and Taft, for the faculty: neither of them an exemplary teacher, scholar, or human being. The only professors who command any respect are dead: the legendary McBee, and Patrick Sullivan (who taught at Ohio State).

Perhaps this is the place for a word on the moral landscape of *The Rule of Four.* Francesco Colonna was a hero of sorts, for he saved treasures from destruction and wrote an immortal work of literature to go along with them. But he was also ruthless to his associates and anyone else who got in his way. The end, to him, justified the means. Richard Curry was also a murderer twice over, but he killed men who were planning to do the dirty on Paul, his beloved surrogate son. The same morality applies in his case. The Sullivans, Paul Harris, Gil Rankin, and Katie Marchand are averagely good people, loyal to their friends and well-disposed to the world so long as their own concerns are not interfered with. Of the villains, Bill Stein is a weak and damaged character looking out for his own career. Vincent Taft is drawn with a broader brush: a difficult man at the best of times, he carries the weight of his academic failure like a deformity. As he flagellates the Good Friday audience with his sadistic imagery, he arouses the pity and terror of a tragic hero. In contrast to all of these is the only Christian among the major characters: the Catholic Charlie Freeman, who risks his life and nearly loses it to save his friend Paul.

Princeton Art Museum

Blair Arch

Firestone Library

Princeton Chapel

Institute for Advanced Study

Ivy Dining Club

Dod Hall

McCosh Hall

Nassau Hall

Princeton photos courtesy of Maya Shmuter

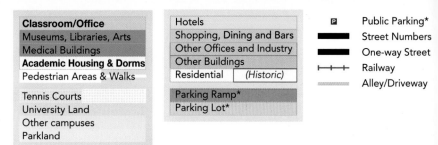

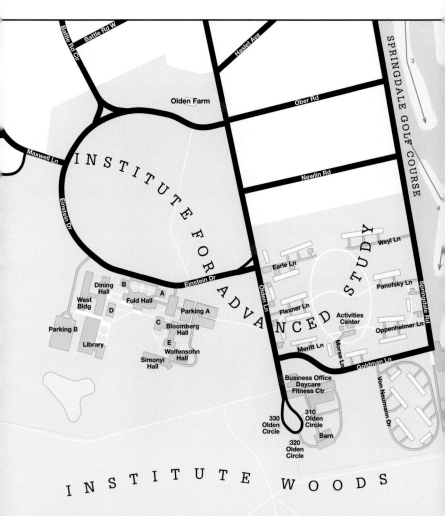

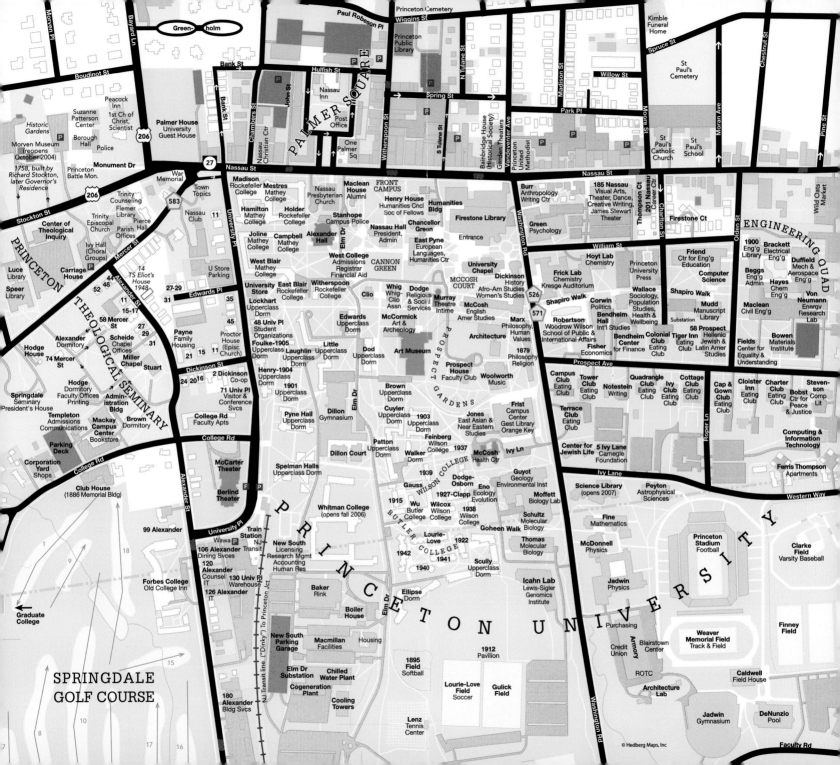

While Greek drama gives this layer of the plot one of its guiding principles, another comes from the symbolism of the Christian calendar. The narrator mentions at the very beginning that it is Good Friday, the day that commemorates the Passion of Jesus Christ. In the Passion story told in the Gospels, three people die: Jesus, and the two thieves crucified with him. In *The Rule of Four*, the three deaths are those of Bill Stein, perhaps cast as the Good Thief (see Luke 23:39-43); Vincent Taft, definitely the Bad Thief; and Richard Curry, who goes to his death willingly, if unnecessarily, for the sake of Paul Harris. Paul, however, is seen by his friends as the real sacrifice of this Passover season.

If this Christian interpretation seems far-fetched, one need only look at the end of the story to see that it is intentional. On p. 351, Tom mentions "my brother Paul, sacrificed on Easter." While the friends sleep, "Charlie fingered the crucifix around his neck." And starting on Easter Sunday morning, April 4, 1999, "we all invested ourselves in the myth of [Paul's] survival, the myth of his resurrection." But there may be yet another sense in the symbolism, for Paul survives his near-death experience and reappears to continue a secret life on earth with his "disciple" Tom Sullivan. Just so, certain Gnostic sects believed Jesus to have survived the crucifixion and lived on as a normal man.

LAYER II. OHIO, CHICAGO, NEW YORK, ITALY, PRINCETON, TEXAS, 1946-2004.

The second layer of the novel is told in the past tense, and fills in numerous facts from the past of Tom Sullivan, his father Patrick, and other characters. After the events of the first layer conclude on p. 350, the reader will notice the shift to the past tense as Tom's history is brought up to the present. The time of his decision to change his life (summer 2004) coincides tidily with the publication of the novel—and with the change that it has presumably wrought in the lives of its authors.

Sufficient information is scattered throughout this layer to enable one to reconstruct the chronology of the Sullivan family, adding considerably to the interest of the story. Here is an account of the main events of Patrick Sullivan's life, which like that of any scholar include the publication of his books and articles. The events of his son Tom Sullivan's life overlap with them and continue the story. The pages of *The Rule of Four* that disclose these events are given in brackets. The earlier dates are conjectured by calculating from two landmarks: 1) The last year of compulsory chapel attendance for Princeton undergraduates (1964/65); 2) The first class of undergraduates that included women (1968/69).

1946:   Early September: Patrick Sullivan born in Columbus, Ohio, son of a bookseller. [38, 70]

1964:   The day after his 18th birthday, enters Princeton.
          His class is the last to attend compulsory chapel. [38]
          At Princeton, becomes best friends with Richard Curry. [61, 62]

1968:   Graduates at the end of the academic year before women students arrive at Princeton. [38] Enters Ph.D. program at University of Chicago. [39]

1969/70: A year of fellowship work researching in New York City. [39, 65] Curry introduces him there to Vincent Taft. [61]

1970:   On a visit home from New York City, meets his future wife, a student at Ohio State University, Columbus. [39, 69]

1973:   Three years after leaving New York City, marries and settles in Columbus. [70] Wife works as an accountant, then takes over the Sullivan bookstore. [39]

1974:   Ph.D. awarded for a dissertation on Renaissance Italy. [39] Hired into tenure/track position by Ohio State. [39] *The Rome of Raphael* published. [46] Dates unknown: daughters Sarah, Kristen born. [14, 40]

1977:   Summer [13, 40]: son Thomas Corelli Sullivan
         born. [40]

1979:   *Ficino and the Rebirth of Plato* published. [46]

1986:   *The Men of Santa Croce* published. [46]

1987:   June: "The *Hypnerotomachia Poliphili* and the Hiero-
         glyphics of Horapollo" published in *Renaissance
         Quarterly.* [46]

1989:   "Leonardo's Doctor" published in *Journal of Medical
         History.* [46]

1991:   "The Breeches-Maker" published in *Journal of
         Interdisciplinary History. [46]*

1992:   Article (written in 1991) published in *Bulletin
         of the American Renaissance Society.*

1992:   Spends summer researching in Europe. Tom, just
         turned 15, accompanies him. [40] Discovers the
         "Belladonna Document" in a Vatican library. [41]

1992-93: Tom's sophomore year of high school. [46]
         The Belladonna Document written, published,
         and reviewed. [47, 43]

1993:   Summer: not long after Tom's 16th birthday,
         Patrick Sullivan dies in a car accident. [13, 47]

1995:   Fall: Tom Sullivan enters Princeton as a freshman
         in the Class of 1999. [5]

1999:   April 2-3: events of *The Rule of Four.*
         May: Tom graduates, spends summer at home
         in Columbus. Goes to work for a computer
         company in Austin, Texas. [359-360]

2000-03: Summers: in three of these years, Tom returns
         to Princeton for class reunions. [358-359]

2003:   Summer: Tom last sees Katie on his 26th birthday. [361]

2004:   Summer: Tom quits job on the eve of his fifth
         reunion [363]; receives package from Paul and
         prepares to leave for Italy. [364, 368]

LAYER III. GENOA, ROME, FLORENCE, 1497-1500.

The third layer of *The Rule of Four* tells the story of Francesco Colonna in his own words. This is found, set off in italics, on pages 157, 207-8, 211-12, 236-37, and 240. Much of what follows will be devoted to explaining and commenting on it.

Chapter 3
Who wrote the Hypnerotomachia?

We now move into the fascinating territory where fact and fiction blur. The *Hypnerotomachia* of *The Rule of Four* is not the real *Hypnerotomachia,* nor is the Francesco Colonna of *The Rule of Four* the real Francesco Colonna. The real book, I am sorry to report, does not contain a coded history, nor did its author immolate himself to save the legacy of Renaissance humanism. Of that we can be absolutely certain. But what is the real *Hypnerotomachia,* and who really wrote it? The book itself indulges in several forms of deception, which is not surprising since it says at the outset that "all human things are but a dream."

Just as a myriad readers of *The Da Vinci Code* naïvely believe that the Priory of Sion really existed and that people like Isaac Newton and Claude Debussy were its Grand Masters, so *The Rule of Four* has given enormous weight to a mistaken identification. As if that were not enough, a prize-winning scholarly book has recently propagated an equally implausible theory of the *Hypnerotomachia's* authorship. The purpose of this chapter, dry and factual as it may be, is to set the record straight by calling on the best scholarly authorities: the Italians themselves, who have been reading and studying the *Hypnerotomachia* for centuries.

UNCONTESTED EVIDENCE

THE DATE. The *Hypnerotomachia* presents itself from beginning to end as the work of its narrator Poliphilo, who signs off at the end with the words: "At Treviso, while unhappy Poliphilo was engaged in the beauteous bonds of love for Polia. 1467, the 1ˢᵗ of May." Literal-minded readers, including Professor Vincent Taft (more on him below) have taken this to be the true date of the work's completion, but it was not so, at least not regarding the *Hypnerotomachia* as a whole.

Here are some of the proofs. The first book makes ample use of Leon Battista Alberti's treatise on architecture, which was not known in Venice before 1480. (P&C, II, p. 7. For explanation of these abbreviated sources, see the Bibliography.) As Paul Harris discovers when he responds to Taft's challenge (*ROF,* p. 140), it also draws on the *Cornucopia,* a lexicon completed in 1479 and published ten years later by Niccolò Perotti. Most strikingly, the author of the *Hypnerotomachia* makes use of Germanicus's *Aratea,* which was first published by Aldus Manutius in 1499 from a manuscript "newly discovered in Sicily." (P&C, II, pp. 14, 288) So the author must have been adding to the book right up to the year of publication and perhaps even during printing.

THE PRINTER. The *Hypnerotomachia*'s printer himself came within a hair of being anonymous. At the very end of the book there is a closely-printed page of errata and their corrections. The last line reads: "Venetiis Mense decembri. M.ID. in ædibus Aldi Manutii, accuratissime," i.e. [printed] "in Venice in the month of December 1499 in the establishment of Aldus Manutius, most accurately." Aldus Manutius (1450-1515), the Latinized form of Aldo Manuzio, was one of the most famous and prolific printers of his time, specializing in religious and classical works (he invented the pocket edition, a great boon to students), and he normally advertised his name on the books that issued from his press, rather than sneaking it in small print onto the errata

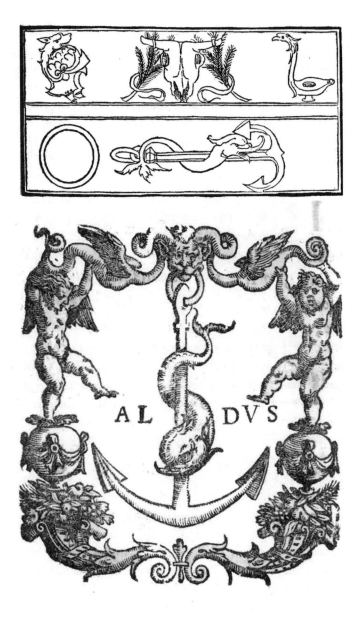

page. The most plausible explanation for this self-effacement is that the *Hypnerotomachia* was not commissioned by Aldus, who typically employed scholars to prepare editions of Latin and Greek texts, but that it was done on a jobbing basis for a private client. Nevertheless, Aldus henceforth adopted a "hieroglyph" from the *Hypnerotomachia* as his printer's symbol: the dolphin and anchor, associated with the motto *Festina lente,* "hasten slowly." [Ills. 21, 22, p.71]

THE CLIENT. The private client introduces himself in the first words of the book after the title-page: "Leonardus Crassus." Also known as Leonardo Grassi, Grasso, Crassi, or Crasso, he was a member of an important family of Verona. He had studied at the University of Padua and become an "apostolic protonotary," i.e. one of the seven principal notaries of the Roman Curia, who registered all the acts issuing from the Vatican bureaucracy. He also held the posts of Captain of the Citadel of Verona and Intendant of the Fortifications of Padua. Like other patricians of his day, he was involved in both church and military affairs. Grassi raises the curtain of the *Hypnerotomachia* with an eloquent letter of dedication to Guidobaldo da Montefeltro, Duke of Urbino from 1482-1508, with whom the Grassi family shared military as well as cultural interests. (A&G, II, p. 493) Guidobaldo, for his part, was the son of the famous learned condottiero (mercenary captain), Federigo da Montefeltro, whose palace in Urbino was a center for humanism and a showpiece of the new style of architecture. The life that was led at his court became the inspiration and model for *The Book of the Courtier,* by Baldassare Castiglione: the ultimate guide to etiquette and the desirable accomplishments of a Renaissance gentleman. The *Hypnerotomachia* could not have been better directed.

But why was Leonardo Grassi dedicating someone else's book? In his dedicatory epistle to Guidobaldo, Grassi explains that "There has recently come into my hands a somewhat novel and admirable work of Poliphilo (for such is the name of the book), which, in order that it shall not remain in darkness, but be of timely benefit to mortals, I have had printed and published at my own expense." (*HP*, p. 2)

Grassi's act of generosity earns our thanks, for otherwise the *Hypnerotomachia* might have been sunk without trace. Priced at one ducat (a gold coin weighing 1/10 oz.), it was not expensive, but it did not prove a good investment for him. Ten years later, in 1509, Grassi addressed an appeal to the Council of Ten (the governing body of the Venetian Republic) explaining that he had spent some hundreds of ducats to print *Poliphilo* "for the public benefit," but because of wartime disturbances, he had not been able to distribute it, and was still holding almost all of the copies. He asked the Council for a privilege prohibiting others from printing or selling the book for ten more years. (C&P, I, p. 153)

THE PUBLICATION. The first edition of the *Hypnerotomachia*, never large, was eventually exhausted. Fortunately the Aldine Press had stored the woodblocks somewhere, so that they could be used to print a second edition in 1545. Only eight of the illustrations had to be replaced, though the entire text was reset in slightly smaller type. Unscrupulous book-dealers have been known to throw away the errata page at the end of the second edition and pass it off as the more valuable first. The book had already found an appreciative audience in France, and in 1546 a group of French humanists produced an abridgement of the text in their own language, at the same time commissioning an entirely new set of woodblocks for the illustrations. These were mostly identical in content, but quite different in style from the illustrations of the Aldine edition: the buildings are shown in greater detail, and the figures have the more slender proportions that were favored by the French artists of mid-century.

To complete the publishing history in brief: the French translation was reissued in 1554 and 1600, the last time with an introductory essay by Jacques Gohorry that interprets the whole novel as a treatise of alchemy. The work was known, after a fashion, in Shakespeare's England, for Sir Robert Dallington, a courtier of Elizabeth I, published an abbreviated English translation of the first third of the *Hypnerotomachia* in 1592. Apart from a reprint by the Bodoni Press of Parma in 1811, nothing more appeared until the complete French translation by Claude Popelin in 1883; the complete Spanish translation by Pilar Pedraza in 1981; the complete Italian translation by Marco Ariani and Mino Gabriele in 1998; and the complete English translation by the present author in 1999. All of these modern versions proclaimed the name of the author to be Francesco Colonna.

THE ACROSTIC. The author desired to remain anonymous, but he could not resist planting four hints as to his identity. Consequently, as early as the 1500s some people knew the secret. The first hint resides in the decorative initial letters that head each of the 38

chapters, and contrast so prominently with the prevailing type. Paul Harris demonstrates this by sticking the letters together, like newsprint in a ransom note (*ROF*, p. 145): they spell POLIAM FRATER FRANCISCVS COLVMNA PERAMAVIT. [Ill. 23, p.74] This translates as: "Brother Francesco Colonna very much loved Polia."

The earliest evidence for the discovery of this acrostic was in a copy of the *Hypnerotomachia* in the library of the Dominicans of the Zattere, Venice, seen in 1723 by the writer and opera librettist Apostolo Zeno. (The book is no longer there.) Some sleuth had written there in Latin: "1512, 20th June. The true name of the author is Franciscus Columna of Venice, who was a member of the Order of Preachers and, being ardently in love with one Hippolyta of Treviso, changed her name to Polia and dedicated the book to her, as we see. The chapters of the book show this through the first letter of each chapter; thus put together they say: 'Poliam frater Franciscus Columna peramavit.' He now lives in Venice at SS. Giovanni e Paolo." (C&P, I, p. 63)

OTHER HINTS. Secondly, the front matter of the book, following the common custom of the time, contained two poems in praise of the work, and both contain clues. One of them, by a certain Matteo Visconti of Brescia, includes the line: "Mirando poi Francisco alta columna/Per cui phama imortal de voi rissona" i.e. "Admiring Francesco, the high column, through whom your immortal fame resounds." (*Colonna* is Italian, and *columna* is Latin, for "column"—a suitable surname for an architectural enthusiast!) Matteo's little poem must have been thought too revealing of the author's anonymity. The relevant page was reset during printing, for the poem is lacking in almost all the copies of the book. The *Hypnerotomachia* copy of the Berlin State Library survives with it intact. (C&P, I, pp. 94-95)

Thirdly, there is a hint concealed in another laudatory poem, this time by Andrea Marone. The poet asks the question: "Who is really called Poliphilo?" The reply is "Nolumus agnosci," "We do not wish to tell," which the ingenious Marco Ariani, latest editor of the *Hypnerotomachia*, spotted as an anagram of COLUMNA GNOSIUS. "Gnosius" means "of Knossos," the ancient capital of Crete, which according to some classical authors was the earliest site of the cult of Aphrodite, or Venus. It was thus an appropriate epithet for the author, a devotee of the goddess. (A&G, II, pp. 495-496)

Lastly, the penultimate page of the *Hypnerotomachia* (before the errata) contains an "Epitaph of Polia," whose three lines begin conspicuously with the letters F C I. Those already wise to the secret will suspect that they spell "Franciscus Columna Invenit," i.e. "Francesco Colonna Invented [this]."

On these grounds, a very strong case would have to be made for the author's name being anything but Francesco Colonna. But this was a common name in fifteenth-century Italy. The surname Colonna was best known as that of a great Roman clan, but people in all walks of life bore it. Which of them was the author? For thirty years, the scholarly field has been the scene of a battle of words between two different views of the matter.

BROTHER FRANCESCO COLONNA, DOMINICAN FRIAR
STATEMENT OF THE CASE. The note recorded by Apostolo Zeno unambiguously identified Francesco Colonna as a member of the Order of Preachers, i.e. a Dominican monk or friar, and said that in 1512 he was still living in the monastery of SS. Giovanni e Paolo in Venice. Now a public hospital, this was one of the largest monasteries in the city, with a magnificent Gothic church dedicated to the saints John and Paul.

Even among the Dominicans of Venice, there were several Francesco Colonnas, but Italian scholars, notably Maria

Theresa Casella, have identified the friar whom they believe to be the author of the *Hypnerotomachia*.

HIS LIFE. Here, summarized from M. T. Casella's volume of documentary biography, are the principal known events:

1433:   Birth, conjectured from the record of his death in
          1527 at the age of 94.
1465:   Priest of the Dominican Order at San Nicolo,
          Treviso.
1467:   Teacher of the novices at Treviso. Periodically found
          at the monastery of SS. Giovanni e Paolo, Venice.
1473:   Incorporated at the University of Padua, as Bachelor
          of Theology.
1477:   Expelled from SS. Giovanni e Paolo and the city
          of Venice, under threat of arrest and incarceration,
          for reasons unknown.
1481:   Awarded the degree of Master *per bullam,* i.e. by decree
          rather than by examination. The Prior of the monastery
          is ordered to pay him 10 ducats on the occasion. Resident
          henceforth at the monastery of SS. Giovanni e Paolo,
          with occasional visits to Treviso. Granted permission
          to travel alone.
1488/93: Preacher at St. Mark's, Venice. At some time, Prior of
          the monastery.
1496:   Released from the post of Prior.
1498:   Syndic and Procurator of the monastery.
1500:   Granted permission to live outside the monastery.
          Asks for a refund of his expenses for making
          the doors of the Choir while he was Sacristan.
1501:   Ordered to repay the sum provided by the Order
          for the printing of a book.
1501/10: Probable period of the composition of the epic

Italian poem *Delfili Somnium* (first published 1959 in Casella and Pozzi's *Opere*), which some attribute to Colonna.

1504:   Votes against the nomination of a Sub-Prior who is supposed to improve the morals and discipline of the monastery. Outvoted, Colonna walks out of the assembly.

1511:   Commissioned to make a silver crown for an altar-statue of the Virgin.

1515:   Leaves Venice, probably as result of economies forced on the monastery. Resides at the monastery of Treviso.

1516:   Visits Venice, perhaps for medical reasons since he is often mentioned in monastery records as being ill. Issues an anonymous denunciation of some colleagues, accusing them of sodomy and other unspecified things. Under investigation by the General of the Order, he confesses his authorship of the calumny and asks pardon. He is banished from Venice to Treviso for life, and forbidden to say Mass or hear confessions.

1516:   Paid the usual fee for saying the first Mass of the day.

1519:   Reinstated at SS. Giovanni e Paolo, Venice. Serves as Master of Grammar, Custodian of S. Nicolò, Procurator.

1522:   Censured for administering the sacrament to a noblewoman against Apostolic Orders.

1523:   Granted allowance of food and firewood on grounds of old age and poverty.

1524:   Denounced on indeterminate grounds by Pietro Britti, a jeweller banished from the city.

1527:   Dies, either in July or on October 2.

A monk is by definition subject to the vows of poverty, chastity, and obedience, but there is little sign of any of them here. Paul Harris says that Francesco Colonna's biography "reads like a rap sheet." (*ROF*, 42), though the resilience of the long-lived and ornery friar is remarkable, as he seems to oscillate between disgrace and privilege. Evidently one could get away with a lot in those days. For all the reputation of the Dominican Order as *Domini canes* (the hounds of God) and zealots of the Inquisition, life in their unreformed monasteries was comfortable and discipline very lax. The monks actually had to be paid to say Mass, which one would think part of their *raison d'être*. They also got around: as we can see, Francesco trotted to and fro between Venice and Treviso, and lived for at least some years outside his monastery, presumably in a rented apartment. When there was a threat to reform the institution, he was very much against it. His brethren enjoyed many years of this way of life, and Paul Harris is correct in saying that when in 1531 Pope Clement VII attempted to force proper monastic observance on them, they retorted that they would rather become Lutherans! (*ROF*, p. 42; C&P, p. 25)

Even so, the harvest of information here, though culled with great labor from Venetian and other archives, is scanty. Little seems to identify Francesco as a writer, let alone a writer of such an extraordinary breadth of learning and emotional depth as the *Hypnerotomachia* testifies to. However, there are a few significant hints, beside the obvious fact that Francesco was not a model monk. His only extra-curricular activities concerned artistic work: the making of doors and a crown, which reflect, in however small a way, Poliphilo's obsession with beautiful buildings and rich objects. There is also the vital evidence that at some time before 1501, Francesco was granted a loan for the printing of a book. The date perfectly fits the *Hypnerotomachia*, published in December 1499 and necessarily in preparation for a couple of years previously. By 1501, Francesco's monastic superiors would have thought it time for sales to have produced some profit, and to call in their loan. Incidentally, this would show that Leonardo Grassi was not quite accurate in claiming to have financed the book on his own, but to have stated otherwise would have threatened the author's anonymity. The expenses of publication, especially the woodcuts, must have been so great that they were probably shared by author and patron, in the vain hope that the dedicatee would cover them with a munificent gift.

A MONK AS AUTHOR?! Was Brother Francesco recognized as an author? Leandro Alberti, author of a 1517 book on illustrious members of the Order of Preachers, mentions him among a group of Dominicans given to humanist studies: "Francesco Colonna of Venice… truly displayed his various and multiple ingenuity in a certain book written in the mother-tongue…" There is some reticence here, as though, observing the author's desire for anonymity, the book is not to be named, though its identity would be clear to those in the know. (A&G, II, p. lxviii)

A year later, in 1518, a sixteen-year-old novice in Francesco's convent inscribed a sonnet in a copy of the *Hypnerotomachia* (discovered by E. Fumagalli in the Cambridge University Library). He addressed the "most elegant book" and said that "Francesco, firm column of virtue, wrote you." (A&G, p. lxix) These two instances, happening a year apart and with Francesco still alive, strongly suggest that his book was known and appreciated on his own territory, and, surprisingly enough, that adolescents were allowed to read it.

At the time, it was entirely normal for boys of intellectual promise but no spiritual inclination to be shoved into a monastery when scarcely able to know their own minds. Likewise, daughters were consigned to convents for life to save their parents from having to find dowries for them. The males, predictably, had a freer time of it. Italian vernacular literature is full of bawdy tales of what they were able to get up to. One such story, by the early 16th century writer Matteo Bandello, tells of a certain "Brother Francesco of Venice who loved a lady, who was in love with another, and tried to have the friar killed; but he killed his rival and left the lady for dead." Although it is fiction, scholars consider it to be strong circumstantial evidence that "our" Francesco was the author's model. The friar of the story lives outside his monastery (as Francesco did); he teaches grammar (as Francesco did) to the nephew of the Doge of Venice, who pays him well; besides, he has money from his family. He buys the young lady many clothes, furnishes her a chamber with beautiful panelling and other decorations, and provides a maid to serve her. So far, Bandello's character accords well with what is known of Francesco the friar: his weakness for women, his appreciation of fine clothes and interior decoration. It is then the novelist's prerogative to build on it a fictional account of murder. At the very least, the story contributes to our picture of the kind of life a friar could lead in late 15th century Venice, and helps to remove the objection that a person in his position could not have been the author of such an erotic and pagan work as the *Hypnerotomachia*. (C&P, pp. 50-61)

While some young men were monks despite themselves, the great monasteries of Italy offered rich opportunities to those of scholarly and intellectual inclinations. The monastery libraries were second to none, and the way of life allowed plenty of leisure for study and creative meditation. It would have been quite possible for Brother Francesco to devote years and years to elaborating his masterpiece. He may well have finished Book II on the stated date of May 1st, 1467, then spent thirty years creating the first and much longer book as his classical erudition accumulated, his vocabulary expanded, and his imagination matured, adding to it as fresh sources arrived at the printing-house of Aldus Manutius, a few minutes' walk away.

This, then, is the case for Francesco Colonna the friar as author of the *Hypnerotomachia*. It is slim evidence, when all is told, but there is nothing implausible about it. Most scholars are content to leave the question of authorship at that.

FRANCESCO COLONNA, LORD OF PALESTRINA

STATEMENT OF THE CASE. In 1965, the art-historian Maurizio Calvesi published his first article identifying Francesco Colonna, the author of the *Hypnerotomachia*, as a Roman nobleman who lived from 1453 to about 1517. For over thirty years, as Calvesi's career took him to the summits of Italy's academic, cultural, and museum worlds, he held fast to this thesis, supporting it in numerous books and articles. His campaign culminated in 1996 with a book of nearly 400 pages: *La "Pugna d'amore in sogno" di Francesco Colonna Romano* (The "Strife of Love in a Dream" of the Roman Francesco Colonna). All the following information is condensed from this work.

Calvesi begins his argument by referring to the first French edition of the *Hypnerotomachia*, 1546, in which Jean Martin, the translator, states that the book "was composed in Italian in the year 1467 by a learned gentleman of an illustrious house." Similarly, in the second French edition (1554), Jacques Gohorry says that he thinks *(opinor)* that the author was of the illustrious Roman family that was rival to the Orsini (traditional enemies of the Colonna clan).

Calvesi's next piece of evidence concerns Leonardo Grassi, who as we recall wrote the dedication and financed the production of the *Hypnerotomachia*. Leonardo's brother was married to the daughter of Franceso Colonna's sister, so that he was distantly related to the Roman nobleman.

The expression "high column," which we found in the second "hint" at the author's name planted in the *Hypnerotomachia*, was used by the fourteenth-century poet Petrarch in a poem dedicated to a member of the noble Colonna family. Calvesi adds several other instances of poems that play on the family's name, and finds similar expressions in the book. He also pursues the theme of the *Hypnerotomachia*'s use of imagery and expressions from Petrarch, emphasizing the poet's connections with the noble Colonnas.

One of the heraldic emblems of the Colonnas was the crowned siren. There is a siren pictured in the *Hypnerotomachia*, but she does not have a crown. [Ill. 24, p.83] Calvesi's explanation is that for her to have had a crown would have made the connection with the Colonnas too obvious, and risked the author's anonymity. At this point I must raise my hand to ask whether, if the siren had had a crown, Calvesi would have taken that as stronger evidence still. (Incidentally, the crowned siren is now universally recognized as the trademark of a coffee company, though modern prudery has cut her off at the waist.)

To continue with Calvesi's arguments: numerous other members of the Colonna family, from the 14th to the 17th centuries, had literary leanings, and Francesco himself occasionally wrote verse, though none of it survives. The Colonnas were also interested in antiquarian matters, and some of them even produced drawings on similar subjects to those of the *Hypnerotomachia*.

The poem of Andrea Marone preceding the *Hypnerotomachia* refers to some kind of "rabid malice" as the reason for not revealing Poliphilo's true name. This could refer to the Colonna family's repeated quarrels with the Popes, which date back to the 11th century and were still going on in 1499.

Leonardo Grassi, in his dedicatory letter, mentions a brother who died on the field of battle in 1496. Captaining the army was Francesco's cousin Prospero Colonna (not the same as his uncle, the cardinal of the same name). Coincidence?

I am attempting to do justice to Calvesi's arguments, though necessarily abbreviating them from a book of nearly 400 pages. But the more baldly one states them, the less impressive they seem. There are numerous similar instances among the 75 pieces of evidence that Calvesi presents, but I move on now to another category of his arguments.

Francesco's properties included the site of the ancient Temple of Fortune, a massive complex of buildings around which the town of Palestrina had grown up (the famous composer Giovanni Pierluigi da Palestrina was born there in 1526). The temple had fallen into ruin, but Francesco undertook its restoration as an act of piety towards antiquity and for the glory of his family name. Perched on a hillside, its most striking features were a series of symmetrical staircases, approaching alternately from left and right, and a grand hemicycle (semi-circular enclosure) in the center. Ancient writers also mentioned a great mosaic which depicted the animals of the Nile and the customs of the Egyptians: it was discovered after 1500. This can all be seen today, for Francesco incorporated the ruins of the temple into a Renaissance palace, and the mosaic, after many vicissitudes, is back in its original home. The relevance of this is that, according to Calvesi, the pyramid-portal that Poliphilo discovers early in the *Hypnerotomachia* is based on the Temple of Fortune, and that many details in its description recall the location and structure of the Palestrina edifice. Moreover, the book mentions Palestrina three times under its Latin name of Praeneste; and three times it mentions the flood of the Nile, which is the theme of the mosaic.

Other connections between the *Hypnerotomachia* and the region of Palestrina include the fact that some of the same plants and trees flourish in both places; and that many of the antique statues and images mentioned in the book have their parallels in the region of Rome. There, too, one finds the greatest collection of ancient inscriptions, such as the book makes use of; and some of them are even bilingual.

The banquet at the court of Queen Eleutherylida has many similarities with a famous banquet held in Rome in 1473, on the occasion of a visit by Eleonora of Aragon, daughter of King Ferdinando. It seems strange, writes Calvesi, that a friar in Venice should have known so much about it, whereas members of the Colonna family were definitely among the guests. Also, many parallels can be drawn between the fictitious Queen Eleutherylida and Cardinal Bessarion, who was actually resident at the palace where the banquet was given. For instance, Bessarion's secretary Perotti compiled the *Cornucopia* from which the author of the *Hypnerotomachia* took many unusual words; and Bessarion's writings treat of some of the same topics as arise in connection with the fictitious queen, such as free will, the Trinity, and the nature of universal intelligence.

The longest argument of Calvesi's work concerns the illustrations of the *Hypnerotomachia* and their similiarities of theme and detail with Roman works, especially the wall-paintings by Pinturicchio in the Borgia Apartments of the Vatican and in the Palazzo Colonna. Calvesi's presentation of the images side by side is, at first sight, impressive. He argues that the designer of the illustrations must have known the Borgia frescoes, which were painted between 1492 and 1494. Pinturicchio, in turn, must have known the book, because around 1503 he painted two versions of the satyr and the sleeping nymph in the Piccolomini Library in Siena. Moreover, the marked interest of the *Hypnerotomachia* author in things Egyptian (especially hieroglyphs) was shared by the Borgia pope Alexander VI, who commissioned Pinturicchio's frescoes.

As for why a noble Roman should call himself *"Frater Franciscus,"* Calvesi expands on Francesco's career. He was apparently an apostolic protonotary, like Leonardo Grassi, and a canon of several churches. Hence he was sometimes addressed as "reverend father," so he was at least in minor holy orders (though canons did not have to be ordained as priests). But more likely, says Calvesi, the "Frater" in the concealed acrostic denoted a fraternal organization, suggesting that Francesco was an initiate of the Roman Academy of Pomponio Leto (see Chapter 4). Everything in the *Hypnerotomachia* seems in accord with the antiquarian and philosophical, even paganizing attitudes, of this academy. The fact that it was suppressed in 1468, however, makes 15-year old Francesco an unlikely "brother." He would have to have belonged to the cleaned-up version of the academy that was revived in the 1480's.

Nearing the end of his arguments, Calvesi tackles the problems of the *Hypnerotomachia*'s all-too-plain connections with the Veneto (the region around Venice). Polia, for example, describes a very realistic upbringing in the city of Treviso and its environs. This prompts Calvesi, who is an expert on esoteric currents, to discourse on whether Polia was a real woman or is just a metaphysical symbol, and whether the book bears an alchemical interpretation, such as was suggested in the French edition of 1600. As for the question of why a Roman should have written a book with such obviously Venetian language, Calvesi deals with the problem summarily: the language, he says, is not particularly Venetian, and anyway his Francesco did have connections in Treviso. This bald answer is in strong contrast to the many pages of careful linguistic analysis on the part of the Hypnerotmachia's editors Pozzi and Ciapponi, as they analyze the Venetian word forms that throng the book.

There remains the report of Apostolo Zeno, who transcribed an inscription in a copy of the *Hypnerotomachia* that clearly identified the Venetian friar and even gave his address. Calvesi dismisses this awkward piece of evidence by accusing Zeno of perpetrating a fraud. Why would a writer of no small repute have done such a thing? Mere regional rivalry, says Calvesi: some were claiming that the *Hypnerotomachia's* author came from the city of Treviso, but Zeno wanted him for Venice, and invented the inscription accordingly.

HIS LIFE. Following his 75 arguments and their notes, Calvesi's richly documented book contains a biography of the Roman Colonna whose episodes, as in the case of the Venetian friar, are extracted here:

1453: Born to Stefano Colonna and Eugenia Farnese.

1468: Mentioned in a generic epigram by Paolo Porcari.

c. 1471: A letter addressed to him by Nicola Della Valle mentions his recent visit to Naples. Two further, anonymous epigrams address him as "beardless," and say that Cicero and Virgil have returned in him (i.e. he is a master of Latin prose and verse).

1473: Pope Sixtus IV appoints him apostolic protonotary and canon of the Lateran. Later in the year he becomes canon of Saint Peter's and has the title of "Magister."

c. 1474: Another epigram calls him an "antiquarian."

1482: The Pope appoints him "commander" of the monastery of Santo Pastore in Rieti, and, for reasons unknown, frees him from any ecclesiastical penalties such as excommunication.

His father dies, and he succeeeds to the lordship of Palestrina, Castelnovo, and other feudal properties.

1483:   The Pope summons him to come without delay. Later in the year he is asked to send to Rome the surplus corn from his property.

1485:   Urgently summoned to Rome, in connection with Pope Innocent VIII's war against the Aragons and the Orsini. By this time, Francesco is also governor of Tivoli, but appears to have installed a vice-governor to act on his behalf.

c. 1490: Marries Orsina Orsini. Three children are born: Stefano, Alessandro, and Giovanni.

1493:   Finishes his restoration of the Palestrina temple as a palace, as dated on the portal.

1494:   Living in the nearby castle of Passerano, perhaps because the Palestrina palace is not yet ready for occupation. Involved in another war against the French, and probably in a war between Fabrizio Colonna (his cousin) and the Orsini which lasts until 1498.

1501:   Pope Alexander VI orders the expropriation of the Colonna properties, including Palestrina.

1502:   The Pope restores Francesco's properties.
        Sells the Castle of Penna.

1503:   The Pope sends soldiers to Palestrina to occupy Francesco's properties. Francesco "gives" them to the Pope in return for a pension.
        The Pope dies, and Francesco's properties are restored to him.

1517:   Family settlements of money and properties suggest that Francesco has recently died.

From this it appears that Francesco led a life typical of his caste. He was not the first aristocratic youth whose classical education awoke a nascent literary gift, nor the only one who was lauded by tutors and hungry men of letters seeking to ingratiate themselves with his family. He was quickly shoehorned into the hierarchy of the Church, which used its wealth to dole out canonries (paid positions requiring no pastoral effort) to privileged young men. However, if he used the leisure and intellectual milieu that came with such a position to pursue scholarly or creative work, there is no sign of it.

On the death of his father and his succession to the lordship of Palestrina, he made a radical career change. The continuation of the family line made it imperative that he marry and have children, so he must have received a dispensation that freed him from the obligatory celibacy of holy orders. His heavy responsibilities in administering his domain were increased first by his determination to finish his father's plan of rebuilding the temple-palace of Palestrina, and then by a series of petty wars and quarrels with the Borgia pope and the Orsini. This turbulent period coincided with the years in which the *Hypnerotomachia* must have been finished, drawing at the last moment on recently published Venetian sources, and the negotiations with Aldus Manutius would have taken place. We then have to imagine that Francesco, having completed the writing of the book and overseen its lavish illustration, persuaded his distant relation Leonardo Grassi to pretend that he had discovered and financed it, though the lord of Palestrina was hardly short of a few hundred ducats. Ten years later, with Francesco still alive, Leonardo kept up the pretence with a moaning appeal to the Venetian Council of Ten to help him recoup his losses.

COUNTER-ARGUMENTS. All in all, the biographical facts for the Roman nobleman turn out to be even skimpier than those of the Venetian friar. The Roman Colonna's involvement in contemporary history is undeniable, but there is not the slightest indication of what he was like in his tastes, talents, and character. The Colonnas considered themselves the very cream of the Roman aristocracy, tracing their ancestry to Aeneas, and through him to his mother Venus. There is a tinge of snobbery in preferring such a distinguished authorship: it goes down well in Rome, to this day. There is some resemblance in Calvesi's crusade to the efforts of maverick scholars to credit the plays of Shakespeare to Lord Bacon of Verulam or Edward de Vere, Earl of Oxford, instead of to the lower-class actor William Shakespeare of Stratford.

I revere scholars of Maurizio Calvesi's stature and learn what I can from them, but I am also familiar with the excesses to which a theory can lead when overmuch emotion and ambition are invested in it. Unfortunately Calvesi's great learning, while it spreads a wide net and draws up a multitude of interesting facts, carefully skirts the most essential question: what is there in the Roman Francesco Colonna's life (never mind all his friends and relations, or people who lived 100 years before or after him) to suggest that he was the author of the *Hypnerotomachia?* I admit that there is not much hard evidence in favor of the Venetian friar, but for the Roman I see not a shred.

Neither do the Italian scholars Giovanni Pozzi and Lucia A. Ciapponi, who produced the critical edition of the *Hypnerotomachia* with a volume of commentary in 1968 (revised ed., 1980). Nor do Marco Ariani and Mino Gabriele, who produced the facsimile with a complete Italian translation, introduction, and commentary in 1998. (I note in passing that this magnificent work came too late for the enormous help it would have given me in preparing my own translation.) Both Pozzi and Ariani take issue with Calvesi's arguments, finding them totally devoid of merit. The exchanges between Pozzi and Calvesi are polite: one can tell that these two senior scholars have a long-standing agreement to differ. But Ariani has less patience with Calvesi's obsessive defence of a thesis that should have died a natural death long ago. He writes:

The seventy-five arguments in favor of the Roman Colonna are all either hypothetical or clearly manipulative to make them conform to a pre-established thesis. One thus has the clear impression (which after a more careful examination becomes a certainty) that Calvesi's infatuation with the Roman Colonna is a prejudicial act with fundamentalist overtones. [...] That Calvesi's passion for his thesis has practically blinded him is proven by the high incidence of exegetical errors of every kind. On discovering these, even someone willing to be seduced by such a siren has to pull back suspiciously when he spies, beneath the attractive surface, the all too visible signs of a trick that is not even up to covering the defects of an unsustainable thesis. (A&G, II, p. lxxii)

Among the many objections raised by Ariani to the Calvesi thesis is the absolute silence of the Colonna family after the *Hypnerotomachia*'s publication. Many family members in the succeeding centuries were scholars or bibliophiles, but not one of them saw fit to mention the authorship of their distinguished ancestor, whose anonymity there was no longer any reason to protect. True, the French editions attributed the work to a noble Roman, but this was a reasonable guess since they knew the acrostic, and everyone had heard of the Colonna family. It did not prove inside knowledge of who the author really was. As for all the claimed similarities between things in the book and things Roman, they were no more than the common property of late fifteenth-century humanists. Knowing the classical literature as he did, of course the author frequently mentions Rome, Praeneste, and some hundreds of other places. But if he had been a native of Rome, he would have made far better use of them, just as he would have used as his "mother-tongue" (contrasted with the literary Italian of Tuscany) the Roman and not the Venetian dialect. As Ariani says, "It is incomprehensible that the Roman Francesco Colonna would have been thus alienated from his own linguistic and cultural heritage, sacrificing it in favor of a language and ambience like those of Venice and Padua, which, biographically and culturally, were completely foreign to him." (A&G, II, p. lxxxi)

Giovanni Pozzi, in his reply to the Calvesi thesis, deplores that nowadays "in large sectors more credibility is given to alchemy than to chemistry, more to astrology than to astrophysics" (P&C, II, p. 3*)—an allusion to Calvesi's esoteric interests. To defend the Roman origin, he says,

> Calvesi and Kretzulesco [see below] suppose that the Roman Colonna was a superintendent of architecture merely because he had his own dwelling restored, as if any speculative builder *(palazzinaro)* could consider himself an architect. They suppose that he belonged to Leto's Academy, without using the documentation that [other scholars] brought to the subject. They make him a host and patron of Alberti, without any sign of this in the copious biographies of the latter. They proclaim him a writer on the strength of two epigrams […] but do not take advantage of the poetic eulogies addressed to their Francesco that are found in Kristeller's *Iter italicum,* a resource that even a beginner in humanistic studies knows and has to hand. (P&C, II, p. 6*)

Paul Harris and Tom Sullivan were led to believe from comparing the parallel lives of the two Colonnas that there was no question of it: the Roman Colonna was their man. (*ROF,* p. 42) Well, here is the evidence: judge for yourself.

LEON BATTISTA ALBERTI

STATEMENT OF THE CASE. The next act in the drama of attribution opened in 1976, when Princess Emanuela Kretzulesco- Quaranta published her remarkable study on the *Hypnerotomachia* and its influences, titled *Les jardins du songe: "Poliphile" et la mystique de la Renaissance* (The gardens of the dream: Poliphilo and the mystique of the Renaissance). A year later, the book was honored with a prize by the Académie Française.

Kretzulesco accepted Calvesi's attribution of the work to the Roman nobleman, but expanded it (as some have done with Shakespeare) to a group authorship that included some of the star names of the Italian Renaissance. First among them was Leon Battista Alberti, the original "Renaissance man" who was equally distinguished as an artist, sculptor, classical scholar, architect, horseman, and athlete. Joining him was Giovanni Pico della Mirandola, the boy wonder of Renaissance philosophy who at the age of 21 offered to debate 900 philosophical and religious theses with all comers. Then there was no less than Lorenzo de' Medici, known as "Il Magnifico," head of the Florentine banking house and supreme patron of the arts. A couple of lesser-known names (see below) presumably served as secretaries and gophers to these luminaries.

A "DANGEROUS" TEXT. Later, with the second edition of *Les jardins du songe,* published in 1986, Kretzulesco changed her mind and came down more firmly in favor of Leon Battista Alberti (1404-1472). Prince Francesco Colonna's role was now reduced to that of the "protector" who had saved Alberti's manuscript from destruction after the author's death. Here is the scenario as Kretzulesco presents it:

> Alberti, "first father" of Poliphilo, must have written the Visionary's Archaeological Itinerary [Book I of the

> *Hypnerotomachia*] in Latin before 1464. The need for a new
> transcription in a language invented for the needs of the
> resurrection of Antiquity occurred to him later. In 1466–1467
> he composed the second part of the novel in Florence. After
> Alberti's death in Rome in 1472, Francesco Colonna saved
> the work by his re-transcription, aided in this by Domizio
> Calderini and Gaspare da Verona, the Venetian humanists
> who were teaching in Rome. Aldus Manutius, among others,
> was their pupil. (*Jardins,* p. 139)

That ingeniously skirts the obstacle of the Venetianisms in the
text: they were added by Colonna's assistants. As for the famous
acrostic, Colonna slipped it in during the transcription process
in order to discreetly immortalize his contribution, though that
entailed fudging the opening words of each of the 38 chapters.

A longer version of this imaginary history, from the same
study, introduces some new celebrities into the club:

> This is how we think Poliphilo's work was saved: at
> Alberti's death in 1472, his heir, Bernardo Alberti, took
> possession of all his papers. Those of *De Re Aedificatoria*
> [On Architecture] were published without difficulty in
> Florence, in 1485. But the "dangerous" text of Poliphilo,
> of which two transcriptions existed in the "new"
> language, also arrived in Florence through the care of
> the powerful nobleman Francesco Colonna. The latter
> confided it to Marsilio Ficino, "Academiae Princeps"
> [Head of the Academy] and to Giovanni Pico [della
> Mirandola], who had returned from France. These two
> are known to have gone to Venice during the winter of
> 1491–92 in order to give Aldus texts for publication.
> Among these texts were some compromising ones,
> such as the *De Mysteriis Aegyptiorum, Chaldeorum* [On

the Mysteries of the Egyptians and Chaldeans—by Iamblichus], etc. There they found a patron: Leonardo Grasso, who obtained permission to print from the Venetian Senate. The first printing did not include the four preliminary leaves; it sold so poorly that these explanatory leaves were added to a second printing: the merits and the interest of the book are celebrated by Grasso, Scytha, Marone, and others. (*Jardins,* pp. 216-217n.)

Kretzulesco developed her Alberti thesis further still in an article which sought to explain the letter "b" with which several of the *Hypnerotomachia*'s woodcuts are signed. She believed that it must be the signature of Battista Alberti, thus making this many-talented man responsible for the illustrations as well as for the text. (*Giardini,* 71-107) But the heavyweight scholars, as usual, pour cold water on such an over-neat thesis. They point out that the wood-engravers "b" and ".b."—two different ones, both contributing to the work—have an independent and documented history, and any attempt to identify them with some famous artist (Giovanni Bellini, Jacopo de Barbari, Benedetto Montagna, Bernardino Pinturicchio, etc.) shows a misunderstanding of the workshop practices current at the time. (A&G, II, pp. c-ciii and illustrations)

ANOTHER MOMENT OF FAME. Although Kretzulesco failed to attract followers to her cause, the Alberti attribution was destined for another moment of fame. In 1997 the press of the Massachusetts Institute of Technology published a large-format book by Dr. Liane Lefaivre, Researcher at the Technical University of Delft, Netherlands, entitled *Leon Battista Alberti's Hypnerotomachia Poliphili: Re-Cognizing the Architectural Body in the Early Italian Renaissance.* The typography was a homage to the Aldine original, making an elegant, though modernized, use of shaped word-blocks, capitals, and illustrations integrated with the text.

Lefaivre came to her conclusions independently of Kretzulesco, being aware only of the first edition of *Les jardins du songe.* Her belief in Alberti's authorship stems from what she sees as "a remarkable fit of his talents with those needed to produce such a complex work." She cites Alberti's love of literature and his defense of vernacular Italian language, combined with a fondness for inventing new words and his great erudition in Latin and Greek; his use of Greek titles for his books; his many writings on the theme of love; the common group of twenty-four classical authorities cited in both the *Hypnerotomachia* and Alberti's treatise *On Architecture;* his knowledge of engineering and mechanical devices; and his expertise in geometry, perspective, and surveying. In addition, Lefaivre offers a lengthy analysis of less obvious clues, such as the similarity between how Alberti and the author of the *Hypnerotomachia* conceived of space and movement; and the way this produces not only a unique series of illustrations to the story but a "visual" text. She writes that he "is writing in a verbal medium but thinking in a purely visual one." She also investigates Alberti's biography for clues that might verify his authorship, and addresses the fact that the manuscript was lost, and only published after his death.

Irrespective of whether Alberti wrote the *Hypnerotomachia* or not, the chapters in which Lefaivre advances this argument contain a mass of information and insight that casts light on both Alberti and the enigmatic book. Her presentation of the *Hypnerotomachia* is the liveliest and most sympathetic ever written. She reads it as a book with a message: as a re-cognition of the human body and a re-assertion of its beauty and its erotic nature, after centuries in which the latter has been despised and suppressed. And as attitudes towards the body go, so does architecture, which is the creative extension and magnification of the human body.

In a fascinating interpretation of the evolution of architecture and of architectural perception, Lefaivre outlines the changing attitudes to the physicality of architecture through the Dark Ages ("The Dangerous Body" of Christian asceticism), the early Middle Ages ("The Marvelous Body" of Byzantine decoration and of the Holy Grail myth), the Gothic era ("The Divine Body" of Abbot Suger's light-metaphysics and of the Virgin Mary), and Alberti's time ("The Humanist Body" of architecture made voluptuous for its own sake). She concludes that during the Renaissance there was a crucial change from a "cold" separation of architecture from the human body and its sensations and desires to a "hot" thinking that set individuals free for reflection and identification in new buildings and artifacts.

This may be so. But is it time for librarians throughout the world to reshelve their copies of the *Hypnerotomachia* and amend their catalogues? How viable is the assertion of Alberti's authorship?

COUNTER-ARGUMENTS. Pozzi and Ciapponi, in their edition and commentary, take the Albertian influence generously into account. Pozzi's notes show that the author of the *Hypnerotomachia* quoted liberally from Alberti's *On Architecture,* which was circulating in manuscript at the time of the *Hypnerotomachia*'s writing. But this does not in the least suggest Alberti's authorship of the novel. On the contrary, it points to the differences between master and follower. "Alberti, seized by didactic necessity, is very much more essential and rapid. But Colonna gives vent rather to the artisan's pedantry: he gives the verbal equivalent of a model, a section, a plan." (P&C, II, p. 8) Francesco Colonna, if he was the Venetian friar, was a part-time goldsmith, and his descriptions of precious objects have the finicky, repetitive quality of his craft. But, more to the point, some descriptions are inaccurate, especially when it comes to the measurements and geometry of buildings. With the best will in the world, commentators and translators cannot fathom what he means by some of his descriptions; and the illustrations do not help because they do not always correspond to the text. The author of the *Hypnerotomachia* may have been in love with classical architecture, but he was muddled and incapable of clear, concise description— if indeed that were possible in his contorted, private language.

One turns from the *Hypnerotomachia*'s architectural descriptions to those of Alberti's treatise with the feeling of emerging into light from a thick fog. Here are two examples, one mathematical and one verbal. In Book VII of his On Architecture, Alberti gives crystal-clear instructions for drawing the spiral of an Ionic capital inwards with a compass. (Alberti, p. 207) In the *Hypnerotomachia*, the author gives similar instructions, but as Pozzi says "his spiral goes outwards, making it impossible to contain it in a given space, and he omits the vital piece of information on where to place the point of the compass." (P&C, II, 165) Colonna "vaguely imitates" Alberti's rule, but he was simply not good at mathematics, as can be seen by the mistakes and confusion that beset his efforts. One soon discovers this if one tries to plot the Island of Cytherea or draw the pyramid-portal using Colonna's measurements as guide. (P&C, II, p. 200)

The second example is that the author of the *Hypnerotomachia* fails to accurately recall a passage from Alberti at the very climax of the story. In his *On Architecture,* Alberti mentions a *ferrea cortina,* i.e., an iron cauldron or tripod, that the Samians once sent to Delphi. (Alberti VII, 230) But Colonna compares the curtain of Venus's sanctuary to "the marvelous *cortina* sent by the Samians to Delphi," evidently giving *cortina* its Italian meaning of "curtain" or "veil" rather than its Latin one of "cauldron" or "tripod." (At least he did not make it an "iron curtain.")

Considering these and many other disparities, Lefaivre's "five highly personal and revealing clues that identify the author as Alberti" fail to convince. They are: references in both texts to animals, abundant musical musings, use of Greek names, occurrence of Alberti's emblem of the eye in some of the hieroglyphs, and Poliphilo's costume of cassock and skullcap (supposedly the uniform of the papal abbreviators, of which Alberti was one). Against these there arise a host of objections, chief among them the notion that Alberti, universal genius, would have written a book in which he garbled his favorite subject of architecture.

OTHER CONTENDERS

Mino Gabriele conveniently summarizes the other claimants to authorship of the *Hypnerotomachia.* (A&G, II, pp. lxxxii-lxxxv)

ELISEO DA TREVISO. A Servite friar who lived in Treviso around 1500 has been identified as author by Alessandro Parronchi (1963) and in several publications by P. Scapecchi. The sole evidence is in a book of annals of the Servite Order by A. Giani, published 1618-1622, which called Eliseo "a Poliphilo, most expert in every kind of knowledge; he published that work in Venice with Aldus Manutius in 1500." On the strength of this, some English libraries have amended their catalogues to give Eliseo pride of place as author of the *Hypnerotomachia*, but almost no one else takes it seriously. Mino Gabriele (see above) surmises that the erroneous attribution came about in the following way. Eliseo in his lifetime, on account of his erudition, was known by his brothers as another "Poliphilo," and a century later, a confused tradition (and total ignorance of the book by the monastic historian) made him the author—perhaps to claim him over the rival Order of Dominicans.

FELICE FELICIANO. A Veronese antiquarian, died 1480, was proposed as author in 1935 by the Leningrad scholar A. Khomentovskaia. Mino Gabriele, in rejecting this, generously points out how difficult it was to obtain adequate sources at that time and place.

GIOVANNI ANTONIO CAMPANO. Mentioned by Pozzi. (P&C, II, p. 3*)

A COMMITTEE, consisting of Leon Battista Alberti, Lorenzo de' Medici, Pico della Mirandola, Francesco Colonna (the Roman one), assisted by Domizio Calderini and Gaspare da Verona. This was an interim suggestion of Emanuela Kretzulesco-Quaranta in the first edition (1976) of her *Les jardins du songe,* before she settled for Alberti as author, the rest as readers or assistants, as described above. Gabriele remarks that "The *Hypnerotomachia*, on a serious textual examination and for one who is really able to read the entire book in the original (an enterprise I believe to have been attempted and concluded by few, even counting certain famous exegetes of the book), shows itself as the work of a single hand and does not support improbable "group" stratifications which would be impossible to hide." (A&G, II, p. lxxxiv)

A COMPLETELY UNKNOWN PERSON. According to Lamberto Donati (1962), the book was written in 1467 by someone who for fear of accusations of pagan practices and immorality remained, and remains, anonymous. The name "Francesco Colonna" is purely fictitious, and there is nothing Venetian about the language.

THE FRANCESCO COLONNA OF *THE RULE OF FOUR*
The Rule of Four impresses one with its knowledge of the *Hypnerotomachia*, and no wonder, for Ian Caldwell studied the work in his last undergraduate year at Princeton University under the Renaissance specialist Professor Anthony Grafton. In an interview for BookBrowse.com, Caldwell says that he

wrote a final paper on the *Hypnerotomachia* for a seminar entitled "Renaissance Art, Science, and Magic," and that it was the research for this paper that gave him the ideal historical piece to complete the jigsaw of the novel. It is probably correct to assume that Mr. Caldwell was mainly responsible for the *Hypnerotomachia* lore in *The Rule of Four*.

Anyone who has read the above account of the Roman Francesco Colonna's life has probably come to two realizations. First, it is very improbable that he wrote the *Hypnerotomachia*. Second, the Francesco Colonna presented in *The Rule of Four* led a somewhat different life from the historical one, and came to a very different end. This kind of manipulation of history is the privilege of fiction, as distinct from scholarship, which is obliged to seek and tell the truth. But the attraction of the genre of fiction to which *The Rule of Four* belongs is that it blurs this distinction. It introduces characters who actually lived and died, and decorates its narrative with the appearance of scholarship. While the reader of *The Rule of Four* realizes that the Princeton parts of the story are fictitious, he or she may well be deceived into taking the historical content as true. What is fascinating for a scholar, reading such novels, is to search out the boundary between the real and the imagined.

Several characters from *The Rule of Four* hover in this borderline zone. Tom Sullivan's father, Patrick Sullivan, had a similar experience at Princeton to Mr. Caldwell's. He fell for the *Hypnerotomachia* under the inspiration of a great Professor: the mousy, elephant-eared Dr. McBee (drawn so as to resemble Professor Grafton as little as possible?). Patrick Sullivan was converted to the theory that Francesco Colonna was a Roman nobleman when he came across the letter (the Belladonna Document) in a Vatican library: it told of how the nobleman of that name had occasioned the killing of two men. There was nothing in this letter to suggest that the Colonna in question was a writer; but at least this discovery was an exciting addition to the bald narrative that is all historians can offer. Patrick Sullivan assembled the biographies of the two contenders in an appendix to his little monograph, and the contest was over, for him, without a struggle. However, the struggle to persuade the world had only begun. His defense of the Roman Francesco was mocked, quibbled with, and, in that dreadful academic death-sentence, "discredited." Perhaps Professor Calvesi felt the same way when the Poliphilic editors, both old and young, dismissed his thirty-year campaign in words not far different from "a sad and sensational bit of self-promotion." (*ROF,* p. 43)

Vincent Taft, the prime mover in the discrediting of Patrick Sullivan and the Roman Colonna thesis, gives his reason for rejection as the fact that the Roman was only fourteen when the *Hypnerotomachia* was written. (*ROF,* p. 140) Perhaps he was a fundamentalist believer in the date of 1467 affixed to the end of the book; but more likely, in challenging his pupil Paul Harris to "shrug off this problem of Colonna's age," Taft was already sensing the possibility of stealing this brilliant protégé's research. Paul, as we know, adheres strongly to the Roman theory because he has long been a fan of Patrick Sullivan's writings. He soon finds proof that whatever the *Hypnerotomachia* says about itself, the book must postdate 1467. (*ROF,* p. 141) In a stunning display of erudition (though easily found if one can read Pozzi's commentary) Paul points out that the author quotes from the *Cornucopia,* a book not published until 1489.

Thirty years before the events of *The Rule of Four,* so in 1969, shortly after graduation, Patrick Sullivan's college friend Richard Curry discovered the manuscript diary of the Genoese portmaster, dated 1497, which told in a crescendo of wonder and interest of a certain Francesco Colonna who was engaged on mysterious shipping business in the port. Eavesdropping on a conversation between this lordly Roman and a Florentine architect, the portmaster heard him tell of "a book he was writing, in which he chronicled the turmoil of recent days." (*ROF,* p. 67) So the Roman Colonna at last acquires one reference to himself as writer of a book, neatly placed two years before the *Hypnerotomachia*'s publication. It is like a mirror-image of the corresponding reference of 1501 in the biography of the Venetian friar.

Tom Sullivan, having lived most of his life in the shadow of his father's obsession, is well up in the matter of the book. *The Belladonna Document* was, after all, dedicated to him as its co-finder. But for the psychological reasons that are beautifully conveyed in the novel, he is equivocal about the whole thing. When he first mentions the *Hypnerotomachia*, in a parody of sloppy student style, he says that it was published "around 1499 by a Venetian man named Aldus Manutius" (ROF, p. 37). It would have been more natural to say "around 1500," but the exact date has been so drummed into him by his father that it slips out! He calls Poliphilo an "allegorical everyman," which is a total misreading of this hyper-sensitive, hyper-educated, hyper-sexed and logorrheic character. But this too is parody.

The two fortuitously discovered documents, which I must emphasize are wholly fictitious, flesh out the hitherto faceless character of the Roman Francesco Colonna. *The Belladonna Document* shows him as ingenious and ruthless; the Genoese portmaster's diary depicts him as a powerful lone wolf engaged in mysterious and secretive activities. Neither one, I have to add, endows him with the particular gifts that it took to write the *Hypnerotomachia*. That comes later, with the full revelation of his coded testament.

Lastly, in another example of the ingenious structure of *The Rule of Four,* Francesco Colonna's life and character are reflected in the person of Richard Curry, the art dealer. Just as Colonna had two men killed in his ruthless quest to preserve the treasures of Renaissance humanism, so Curry kills Bill Stein and Vincent Taft. His motives are to preserve the treasure of Colonna's legacy for his surrogate son, Paul Harris. Both men die by fire, in circumstances both heroic and insane. Colonna dies while trying to pull the treasures out of Savonarola's bonfire; Curry dies in the Ivy Club fire, after giving Paul the all-important blueprint.

But nothing is quite simple here. Perhaps Paul is the real phoenix (see *ROF,* p. 293), returning after 500 years to inherit Francesco Colonna's legacy. Like Francesco's "five close humanist friends" (*ROF,* p. 287), Paul has five people who help him in his obsession. Two of them, Stein and Taft, are murdered for planning to betray him, just as two of Francesco's friends (Rodrigo and Donato) were murdered in the Belladonna incident. That leaves three faithful ones. In Francesco's case they are the brothers Matteo and Cesare, who die with him on February 27, 1498, and the architect Terragni, who survives to complete the *Hypnerotomachia* and publishes it the following year. In Paul's case they are Charlie Freeman and Gil Rankin, who gradually go their own ways after the catastrophe of April 3, 1999, and Tom Sullivan, who remains to complete the story.

It goes without saying that *The Rule of Four* ends on a cliff-hanger. The reader can hardly wait to read the adventures of Tom and Paul as they attempt to open Colonna's crypt.

Chapter 4
Underground Currents and Codes

THE REAL ROMAN ACADEMY

In *The Rule of Four,* Tom Sullivan accepts his father's theory of the Roman Francesco Colonna, persuaded mostly by what he learns about the Roman Academy, "a fraternity of men committed to the pagan ideals of the old Roman Republic, the ideals expressed with such admiration in the *Hypnerotomachia.*" (*ROF,* p. 43). Such a fraternity sounds good enough to be fictitious, but it did in fact exist.

The Roman Academy began around 1450 and flourished in the favorable climate of the humanist popes Nicholas V (ruled 1447–55) and Pius II (ruled 1458–64). It was a loosely constituted group that met at the home of Giulio Pomponio Leto (1424–98), Professor of Rhetoric at the University of Rome and a passionate enthusiast for the Roman past. The members of the Academy were mostly his ex-pupils; Francesco Colonna's name does not appear among them.

Pomponio was a kind of "historical re-enactor." He wore garments resembling Roman dress; he knew all the ancient monuments of Rome intimately, and would guide his guests around them, telling all the stories associated with them and falling into ecstasies of admiration for the great civilization of the past. He shared his modest villa with the historian Bartolommeo dei Sacchi, known as Platina. Here, among his orchards and vegetable gardens, Pomponio emulated the Pythagoreans in following a vegetarian diet, and tried to foster the ideals of the old Roman Republic before it became hypertrophied into the Empire. Many of the academicians also frequented the villa of Cardinal Bessarion, a Greek theologian and philosopher who had been a disciple of the great Platonic revivalist, George Gemistos Plethon. They also visited the Catacombs, the underground burial complexes of Rome, where they wrote their Latinized names on the walls, giving Pomponio the epithet "Pontifex Maximus"—which would later get him into trouble, this being a title of the Pope. Thus there was a kind of Romano-Greek axis in mid-century Rome, uniting those who did not believe that the Judeo-Christian revelation was all in all, but that classical studies were equally worthy of a lifetime's dedication.

Information on what the Roman Academy did at their meetings or underground conclaves is tantalizingly scarce, but what is certain is that it got on the wrong side of Pope Paul II (ruled 1464–71). Rumor had it that the Academicians had become so enamored of ancient Rome that they were conspiring to overturn papal rule and revive the Republic. One rumor led to another. In the words of the Milanese ambassador to the Vatican, writing to his master Galeazzo Maria Sforza:

> For some time now they have had a certain sect consisting of quite a few persons, always growing and including members of all conditions, most of them relatives of cardinals and prelates. They hold the opinion that there is no other world than this one, and that when the body dies, the soul dies, too; and that nothing is worth anything except for pleasure and sensuality. They are followers of Epicurus and Aristippus as far as they can be without making a scandal, not out of fear of God but of the world's

justice, having in all things respect for the body, because they hold the soul to be nothing. And therefore they are given solely to enjoyment, eating meat in Lent and never going to Mass, taking no notice of vigils or of saints and holding in thorough contempt the Pope, the Cardinals, and the Universal Catholic Church. (Calvesi, p. 189).

THE POPE'S LONG ARM. In March 1468 the Pope ordered their arrest. Platina was seized while dining with his young patron Cardinal Francesco Gonzaga. Pomponio was in Venice at the time, but the long arm of papal authority brought him back for interrogation, using as its excuse an accusation of homosexuality. Bessarion was in time to warn some of the other members; one fled to Greece. The charge of heresy was added to that of conspiracy, and the Academicians were imprisoned for about a year and, says Platina, repeatedly tortured, from which one of them died.

The pious papal historian Ludwig Pastor wrote: "There was certainly some ground for the charges brought against the Academicians of contempt for the Christian religion, its servants and its precepts, of the worship of heathen divinities and the practice of the most repulsive vices of ancient times." (Quoted in Palermino, p. 117n.) In other words, they had a low opinion of this Pope and of the conduct of the church, and some of them were homosexual. This seems to have been the extent of their sins, and although their experience was traumatic, none of them was finally convicted—which would have led to the stake—and most were able to continue their careers. Platina, submitting to the inevitable, even became Vatican Librarian. There he enjoyed a scholar's revenge, writing an authoritative *History of the Popes* and damning Paul II for all posterity.

It was not Christian zeal or homophobia that motivated the crushing of the Roman Academy, but a power-play that Emanuela Kretzulesco (*Jardins,* pp. 37-45) attributes to the notorious Borgia family. She tracks their conspiratorial rise, beginning in 1456 when the weak Pope Callixtus III appointed his 26-year-old nephew Rodrigo Borgia as vice-chancellor and cardinal. In 1464 the humanist Pope Pius II died, and before the conclave could be held to elect his successor, two cardinals of the same way of thinking also happened to die, neither of them very old: the gentle and learned Nicolas of Cusa and Cardinal Prospero Colonna, Francesco's uncle. The prudent Cardinal Bessarion left Rome for a monastic life.

These men had always been against the investment of secular power in the Church, which for them served a kingdom "not of this world." With the four of them out of the way, the faction that favored more and more temporal power took over.

When Paul II fired the Papal Abbreviators in 1464, Rodrigo Borgia became Prefect. He persuaded Paul that as the Vicar of Christ, the Pope should wield both temporal and spiritual powers—and cultural ones, too. Under Sixtus IV (ruled 1471-1484), Rodrigo's power grew greater than ever, and under the next pope, Innocent VIII (ruled 1484-1492), another suspicious series of premature deaths began in Florence, seat of the second most powerful family in Italy. Kretzulesco mentions Lorenzo de' Medici's wife Clarice Orsini—the Florentine's invaluable link with Roman society—and her eight-year-old daughter, who both died after returning from Rome (1488); Bertoldo di Giovanni, sculptor and keeper of the Medici sculpture collection; and Lorenzo himself (1492). In Rome, the apostolic protonotary Lorenzo Colonna, a member of the family that had most resisted Borgia policies, had been beheaded in 1484. The Pope himself died of the same "gout" which had carried off many of the aforementioned, and Rodrigo was able to buy sufficient votes to succeed him, as Pope Alexander VI (ruled 1492-1503).

Unexpected death continued to visit the humanists: Ermolao Barbaro died of a "fever" on a visit from Venice to Rome in 1493; the Florentine academician Angelo Poliziano of the same in 1494; Pico della Mirandola in 1494, reputedly poisoned by his secretary. Kretzulesco writes of how many of these premature deaths were blamed on gout, in itself a painful but not generally fatal disease; and of how there was a poison, known to the Borgias, that disintegrated the bones under the semblance of gout. (*Giardini,* pp. 88-89) Be that as it may, the serial deaths in Florence and Rome spelled the end of the two philosophical academies and of the free exchange of ideas for which they stood. It is in this desolate landscape that *The Rule of Four* situates Francesco Colonna, as he contemplates the fall of everything he has lived for and loved.

The only haven where humanists and devotees of the prisca theologia could meet and share their vision of the world was now in the independent republic of Venice. Among the first to take advantage of the cultural climate there was Erasmus of Rotterdam, who worked editing classical manuscripts for the press of Aldus Manutius. The Aldine Press, in fact, became the home of a "Neo-Academia Philellenica" (new Greek-loving academy) and the source of the greatest dissemination of classical literature that had ever been.

FRANCESCO'S CRYPT AND THE ROSICRUCIANS. The most thrilling invention in *The Rule of Four* is the notion that before Francesco Colonna died, he built a crypt or vault in which he secured his collection of classical texts and works of art (*ROF,* p. 285). The idea may have occurred to the authors independently, but there is a decided similarity to the most famous vault in the history of secret societies. A short book called the *Fama Fraternitatis,* written in German around 1609 and published in 1614, told of how in 1604 these Rosicrucian brothers had rediscovered the vault in which the founder of their Order, Christian Rosenkreutz, had been interred 120 years previously.

It was seven sided, lit by a perpetual lamp, and decorated all over with symbolic figures and sayings. In each of the seven walls there was a cupboard containing books of wisdom. In the words of the English translation of 1652, there were also "little bells, burning lamps, & chiefly wonderful artificial Songs; generally all done to that end, that if it should happen after many hundred years, the Order or Fraternity should come to nothing, they might by this only Vault be restored again." (*Fama,* p. 23)

We recall the intention of Francesco Colonna in *The Rule of Four,* who stocked his crypt with representative treasures of humanism, so that whatever happened to him, future ages might be able to restore it.

Beneath the altar in the center of the vault was the uncorrupted body of Christian Rosenkreutz,

> ...a man admitted into the mysteries and secrets of heaven and earth through the divine revelations, subtle cogitations and unwearied toil of his life. In his journeys through Arabia and Africa he collected a treasure surpassing that of Kings and Emperors; but finding it not suitable for his times, he kept it guarded for posterity to uncover, and appointed loyal and faithful heirs of his arts and also of his name. (*Fama,* p. 24n.)

There is no room here for a further digression on the history of the numerous societies and secret Orders that have called themselves Rosicrucian. Some of the more "fundamentalist" ones believe that Christian Rosenkreutz's vault really was discovered as the *Fama* relates, and still exists in a secret location somewhere in Germany.

But the web of connections becomes ever more fascinating when one reads the work in which the character of Christian Rosenkreutz was first invented. It is a short novel entitled *The*

Chemical Wedding of Christian Rosenkreutz, written by Johann
Valentin Andreae (1586-1654) around 1607, though it was not
published until 1616. This brilliant young man had obviously
been delving into the *Hypnerotomachia,* whose influence is evident
throughout his surrealist allegory (the wedding, at which the bride
and groom are beheaded, is really an *alchemical* one). For instance,
Christian Rosenkreutz journeys by sea to a mysterious island
where alchemical rituals of rebirth take place, and on the way is
greeted by a chorus of sea-gods. On the island he illegally enters
an underground crypt, accompanied by a mischievous Cupid,
and there discovers Venus stark naked and asleep.

CODED MESSAGES?

ACROSTICS. The acrostic that conceals, or reveals the name of
the author of the *Hypnerotomachia* belongs to a historical practice
of which Colonna was doubtless aware. Acrostics are words or
word-patterns whose letters occur at regular intervals, such as
the beginnings or endings of lines or verses. The oldest ones are
probably those found in the Hebrew Scriptures (Old Testament).
As many as twelve of the 150 Psalms of David use acrostics,
though these do not spell out words but simply follow the 22
letters of the Hebrew alphabet in sequence. Thus Psalms 9 and
10 (sometimes counted as a single psalm) begin every second
verse with the letters in alphabetical order, and Psalms 25 and 34
every verse. Psalm 119, the longest of all, is the most ingeniously
structured. It consists of 22 stanzas, each containing 8 lines that
all begin with the same letter. The psalm-like Lamentations of
Jeremiah also follows an alphabetical pattern, each of its chapters
having 22 stanzas, one beginning with each letter in turn. The
purpose was probably an aid to memorization.

A famous Greek acrostic occurs in the poem attributed to
the Erythraean Sibyl, one of nine prophetic women whose oracles
were adapted to Christian purposes. The initial letters of the

verses spell out the Greek for "Jesus Christ, God's son, savior," itself an acrostic of the word for "fish," *ichthys.* It is well known that early Christians took the fish as their sacred symbol.

In the Latin world, acrostics were used by Plautus in the prologues to his comedies; in inscriptions; and as a literary game, in which not only the first and last but even the middle letters of each line were employed. More relevant to Colonna's case are the instances in which the acrostic conveys the author's name. One such occurs at the beginning and end of the Latin version of Homer, giving the name of (Silvius) Italicus. Another is in a letter written to the emperor Julian, included in the *Palatine Anthology.*

With such precedents, Colonna's encoding of his name and his love for Polia falls into a distinct, if rare, tradition.

It is another matter with the coded messages that *The Rule of Four* purports to discover in the text of the *Hypnerotomachia.* These belong to a different tradition, that of cryptography or steganography (from Greek "covered writing"), more commonly called codes and ciphers. Its principles also derive from classical antiquity, whose authors told of various ingenious methods by which secret messages had been conveyed. Most of these were quite basic by modern standards, usually consisting of some substitution cipher and easily cracked through knowledge of letter-frequency (see *ROF,* p. 155 for an example). The codes in *The Rule of Four* go beyond the normal ingenuity of the *Hypnerotomachia* period, but they receive some validation from the writings of Abbot Trithemius of Sponheim (1462-1516). Trithemius wrote both a *Polygraphia,* describing a method of universal communication, and a posthumously-published *Steganographia*, a most notorious work in the history of magic. Beside giving examples of many different coding methods, Trithemius's steganography contains a system of secret communication through the invocation of angels. There was, and still is, controversy about whether Trithemius really meant this as an occult and magical procedure, or whether the angels' names were just there to confuse the issue for would-be decipherers. In the sixteenth century, such controversies were a burning issue, because of the fear that someone using Trithemius's system might be contacting not angels but demons. Today the issue is more academic.

PAUL HARRIS, MASTER DECODER. *The Rule of Four* pretends that the *Hypnerotomachia* is a coded text from beginning to end—especially the end, i.e. Book II, completed by Terragni after Colonna's death. Paul Harris's decipherment proceeds through several stages, each facilitated by one of his friends. Since the process is not easily grasped from the fast-moving and conversational narrative, I outline it here.

The first discovery follows logically on the known fact of the acrostic signature of Francesco Colonna. Paul notices (*ROF*, p. 146) that the first of the "Egyptian" hieroglyphs is an eye, which was the chosen emblem of Leon Battista Alberti. This makes him think of Alberti's invention of Latin equivalents for Greek architectural terms, and he realizes that Colonna has done the same thing (which is broadly speaking true). But there is one passage where Colonna leaves the terms in Greek (so Paul says; I would say that Greek terms are scattered throughout among the Latin ones, but let that go). Here Paul substitutes the Latin terms, as Colonna and Alberti normally did, and reads the first letter of each resultant row acrostic-wise. This yields the message: "Who gave Moses horns?"

At this point, Tom Sullivan provides the catalyst by remembering Michelangelo's statue of Moses, with his prominent horns: the result of a mistaken translation institutionalized by Saint Jerome in his Vulgate (Latin) version of the Bible. The word in question is *cornuta*, which Paul sets out to find in the *Hypnerotomachia*. When he locates it, he reads every seventh letter from there onwards, for three chapters. (*ROF,* p. 156) Thereupon Francesco Colonna begins to speak to him across the gulf of time.

Paul next discovers that the varying lengths of the *Hypnerotomachia*'s 38 chapters have a definite rhythm (*ROF,* p. 200), and this alerts him to the points at which a clue is to be found. (In point of fact, the "pulse" is not nearly as regular as is claimed.) Katie is the catalyst here, recalling a game described in Thomas More's *Utopia* of 1516. This enables Paul and Tom to find the right numerical sequence for the decoding of the second message. (See Chapter 6, comment on *ROF,* p. 207, for an explanation of it.)

Tom again turns to Alberti's architectural treatise to help Paul solve the third riddle, which poses a question concerning perspective. The answer is a simple quantity in *braccie,* an Italian unit of measurement, and it yields a cipher based on the first letter of every third word. (*ROF,* p. 211) The fourth riddle is solved by Paul alone, through consulting Horapollo's work on hieroglyphics. This explains what happens to victims of the night-owl, to an eagle with a twisted beak, and to a blind beetle: they all die, and the cipher-word is the Latin for death, *mors.* (*ROF,* p. 236)

The fifth and last of this series of encoded messages depends for its catalyst on Charlie, thanks to his knowledge of medical history. "Where do blood and spirit meet?" asks the riddle. Not in the heart, as many medieval anatomists believed. Francesco's great learning has made him aware of something that would not be generally credited for another hundred years: that they meet in the lung. The Latin term *pulmo* gives the key to Colonna's farewell to his reader, whom he now leaves dependent for decipherment solely on the Rule of Four. (*ROF,* p. 240)

THE RULE OF FOUR AT LAST! The "Rule of Four," which gives the novel its title, has at least three meanings. In the present case, it is the rule of seeking letters in turn from the four directions of space. Obviously it also refers to the four friends, Tom, Paul, Charlie, and Gil. Moreover, those familiar with old-fashioned arithmetic will know of the "rule of three," which enables one, when three numbers are given (a,b,c) to find the fourth term, d, such that a:b = c:d. The "rule of four" perhaps plays on this, being a more complicated formula.

Paul first discovered the rule in the Genoese portmaster's diary, in the form of the directions: *"Four south, ten east, two north, six west, De Stadio."* (*ROF*, p. 170) At that stage, he believed it to be a geographical direction that would lead to the location of Francesco's crypt, working from one of the stadiums of Rome. One immediately notices its redundancy in such a situation: it would have been sufficient to say "Two south, four east." Later, Paul explains to Tom Sullivan that the four directions apply to the *Hypnerotomachia,* each one of them denoting a letter. (*ROF*, p. 272) Once Paul understands how this works, there is no stopping him. He reads the cipher like a book, and races through to the end of Colonna's dramatic tale, and its continuation in the same code by the faithful Terragni.

The first question to arise in the mind of the skeptical reader is whether such encoding is even possible. To answer it, there is no alternative but to try it oneself. Here is an example of the type of cipher that uses the first letter of every third word:

> In a deep abyss, delved by Nature in her colossal bosom, lurked a monstrous form like a winged dragon. Hearing the wheezing and vomiting emitted by its lungs, and the loud clashing of a thousand scales, not even the dread, unnatural basilisk dared penetrate the underground lair of such a monster. To this ghastly, infernal hole came none other than the intrepid Lancelot, his heart fearful of nothing either mortal or immortal. As the dragon saw him, it offered a long, noxious blast.

Using every seventh letter is more difficult, and (at least in the hands of this beginner) produces something horribly like a literal translation of the *Hypnerotomachia*:

> Then, with a bold heart and right sturdy, he flung a spear far down. Ineffable, awful, and most dire, up came a roar.

The code that uses the 3rd, 4th, 6th, and 9th letters in rotation would present much the same challenge. As for the Rule of Four, the authors themselves have demonstrated how it can be made to work in English. (*ROF, pp. 273-274*) None of these methods is impossible, so long as one can conceal the coded message in any amount of verbose rhetoric. But the codes that depend on the first letters of lines would require the author to be constantly attendant at the printing press, to make sure that the compositors put the right number of letters into each line. One can imagine how unwelcome he would have been in Aldus Manutius's busy shop.

The next question is whether such codes exist at all in the *Hypnerotomachia*. I doubt that it contains anything of the kind, beside the acrostic signature. Although I would not swear that the word *cornuta* never appears in the book, I have not found it. (Colonna's usual term for "horned" is *cornigero*.) Nor does the word *stadia* occur near the beginning of the Book II, as Paul claims it does. There is no point in looking for codes, anyway, because the history that is encoded in the *Hypnerotomachia*, according to *The Rule of Four,* is a fictional one. It concerns an imaginary development grafted onto a real person, the Roman Francesco Colonna; it tells of things he never did, and a death he did not die. Moreover, the best scholars reject him as the author of the *Hypnerotomachia*. In short, the whole idea of the coded messages belongs to the fictitious element in *The Rule of Four.* The fact that it is a brilliant idea, and expertly carried out, does not make it the least bit true.

SAVONAROLA'S BONFIRES

As *The Rule of Four* makes plain, the career of Savonarola in Florence was intimately connected with that of the last of the fifteenth-century Medici, Piero di Lorenzo. The facts are these. Girolamo Savonarola came to Florence in 1490, at the age of 38. He was a Dominican, of the same monastic Order as Fra Francesco Colonna, but as different as could be in his reputation for "severe personal piety and fervor." (Meltzoff, p. 32) It was Lorenzo the Magnificent who was rash enough to invite him to the city, and Pico della Mirandola who had advised Lorenzo to do so; thus two of the prime movers of the humanistic Renaissance must take part of the blame for subsequent events. Their motive seems to have been to restore Christian oversight to a Florence whose sins Paul Harris has well described. (*ROF,* pp. 279-280) Savonarola was a republican in politics, a puritan in taste, and a fire-and-brimstone evangelist. Soon "he had attacked the natural sciences, the speculative sciences, the study of law and lawyers, the studies of philologists and grammarians, the study of Greek and Hebrew, and of philosophy in general, and of philosophers in particular, notably the pagan sophistry of the 'chief of this age,' ancient literature, and modern secular studies, and suggested that they should all be banished by Christian rulers whom he attacked for their complacent pride in their own virtue as not fit leaders of a Christian state." (Meltzoff, pp. 43-44)

Lorenzo the Magnificent had reserved the right to expel Savonarola if the friar made trouble; but it was now too late: Lorenzo died in 1492, leaving as heir to the unofficial rulership of Florence his son Piero, aged twenty.

PIERO THE FATUOUS. Piero di Lorenzo (thus named to distinguish him from all the other Pieros in the Medici family) had been educated from the age of three by the humanist Angelo Poliziano. Like Plato pinning his hopes on the young tyrant

Dionysus of Syracuse, Poliziano and his fellow-Platonists thought they had done a good job of training a philosophic monarch. But what if Piero succumbed to Savonarola's influence? That would spell the end of the golden age of Florentine humanism: an age that had seen Poliziano's Orphic drama, Ficino's magical Orphic songs and his Platonic Academy, Pico della Mirandola's attempt to embrace the whole world's wisdom in an esoteric Christian synthesis. It would end the passionate rediscovery of antiquity, and the patronage of living artists whose merits need no underlining. So what did Piero do? He commissioned young Michelangelo to build a snowman.

This unfortunate scion of the Medici did not last long. In 1494, when Charles VIII of France saw his opportunity to further his claims on Italian soil, and his troops approached the city, Piero capitulated. The people of Florence, enraged, expelled him and struck their own deal with the French king. During sixty years of Medici dominance, the city had forgotten how to function as a republic, and so Savonarola became its effective ruler.

Savonarola's chief enemy during his years of triumph was the Borgia Pope, Alexander VI, who repeatedly summoned, excommunicated, and threatened him. The Pope's object seems to have been to reinstate the enfeebled Medici as a puppet ruler, and then to install his own sons. This did not move the Florentines, while the war with France and ensuing famine and plague only strengthened Savonarola's hand. Fear that the Antichrist was shortly to appear, announcing apocalyptic times, was a recurrent feature of the period, and Savonarola exploited it with the perfect sincerity of a fanatic. This is the background against which the famous bonfires have to be seen.

BONFIRE OF THE VANITIES. The term "Bonfire of the Vanities," popularized by Tom Wolfe's novel of that name, is a translation of *brucciamento delle vanità*. Savonarola held two such events in

Florence, on February 7, 1497 and February 27, 1498. (Steinberg, p. 6) Some modern historians keep to the dating system of their fifteenth century sources, for whom the New Year began in March, so that they give the bonfire years as 1496 and 1497 (e.g. Meltzoff, p. 291). In both cases, the date of the bonfire coincided with Carnival, just before the beginning of Lent.

Paul Harris's account of the first fire in *The Rule of Four*, pp. 282-283, is historically accurate. A list of vanities compiled from eyewitnesses comprises wigs, veils, cosmetic colors, perfumes, mirror, and the like; games and gambling instruments; carnival masks and beards; books of music and harps, lutes, cithers, bagpipes, cymbals, horns, and other instruments of uncertain identification; books of poems, both Latin and Italian, including works by Boccaccio, Dante, and Petrarch, and other "indecent" writings; paintings of beautiful figures showing much immodesty; beautiful ancient sculptured figures of Florentine and Roman women; sculptured portraits by the great masters such as Donatello and others; and all indecent paintings and sculpture and prints. A Venetian merchant offered 20,000 ducats to buy the whole lot before it was burned, but the Signoria turned him down.

After the second bonfire, public opinion turned against the friar. Although there was no crime or sin of which he could be justly convicted, a kangaroo court caused this public nuisance to be tortured, hanged, and burned. The whole episode is a depressing one, and nobody comes out of it very well.

Historical judgment of Savonarola tends to vacillate along with the emotions aroused by the paganism of the Renaissance. Marsilio Ficino, who had devoted his life to reconciling Hermes and Plato with Christ, acclaimed Savonarola when he first appeared in 1494, but became personally threatened as the friar ranted against humanism. The Platonic philosopher sulked in retirement until after Savonarola's death, when he was free to pin the label of Antichrist on the friar himself. (See Meltzkoff, pp. 296-302) To the Age of Reason, Savonarola was an example of the dangers of religious enthusiasm, both for the world and for its proponents. The Catholic Romantics of the nineteenth century, on the contrary, regarded the paganizing tendencies as the enemy of a pure, Christian Renaissance, and rehabilitated Savonarola. (See Steinberg, pp. 25-31) Now the pendulum tends to swing the other way.

The Rule of Four avoids both extremes of the pendulum. According to the plot of the novel, Savonarola was the antagonist of Francesco Colonna and the indirect cause of his martyrdom. Yet the friar appears there in a balanced and quite sympathetic light, especially in his last interview with Francesco. (*ROF*, pp. 290-292) Whereas the novel treats Francesco as a largely fictitious character, it presents Savonarola and the historical events around him in a factual way. The friar's bonfires play an essential role in the plot, for without them there would have been no incentive for Francesco to construct his crypt and bury his time-capsule of treasures in it. Nor would he and his companions have met a martyr's end.

THE CURIOUS CASE OF THE PEDNOSOPHERS

DID THE ROMAN ACADEMY SURVIVE? The Platonic Academy of Florence died with Lorenzo de' Medici. Did anything survive of its Roman counterpart after the predations of the Popes and the débâcle of Savonarola? There is tantalizing evidence that it lasted in some form for another three centuries.

In the mid-nineteenth century, a French historian of Freemasonry, J. M. Ragon, translated a manuscript which told of a so-called "Pythagorean Order" that had led an underground existence ever since the fall of the Roman Empire in the fifth century A.D. It is a fascinating document, which to judge by its handwriting dates from between 1700 and 1750.

The title of the Order refers to the early Greek philosopher Pythagoras (6th century B.C.), famous for his mathematical and musical discoveries, for his vegetarianism, his belief in metempsychosis (the rebirth of souls in new bodies), and for giving two levels of teaching: the *exoteric*, available to all, and the *esoteric*, reserved for initiates. Many of these features were taken over by Plato, who founded the first of all Academies as early as 385 B.C.: the School of Athens. Ragon's manuscript begins with the well-known history of this philosophical school, which lasted unbroken for nine hundred years until A.D. 529, when the Emperor Justinian suppressed it along with all pagan institutions. Its last philosophers found a refuge in Persia (now Iran) at the court of Chosroes the Great. Since Islam had not yet appeared, Persia was a Zoroastrian nation, and its wise Magi (the original "magicians") had a great respect for Greek philosophy.

This much is fact, but Ragon's story now diverges from the historical record, though nothing in it is inherently improbable. It tells that these Platonic philosophers were able to return to Greece under the new name of *pednosophoi*, "children of wisdom." But they were now a world-wide Order, with members and influence in what would become the Islamic world, and in the Eastern Christian Empire of Byzantium. Two hundred years after Mohammed, the Caliph al Mamoun (ruled 813-33) welcomed the Pednosophers as part of his effort to revive Greek learning, science, and philosophy among the Arabs. The Order's headquarters were for a while in Damascus, then in Baghdad. The Eastern "Roman" Empire was ruled from Constantinople (now Istanbul, Turkey), where the Order was headed in the eleventh century by Michael Psellus, the greatest Byzantine philosopher and a keen follower of Plato. The Knights Templar came into contact with the Pythagorean Order during the Crusades, and made their own adaptation of its teachings, using different symbols. This started a separate branch of the wisdom tradition that would later emerge as Templar Freemasonry. (Readers of Dan Brown's *The Da Vinci Code* will hear all manner of resonances here.)

In the 1430s, another Byzantine philosopher and politician, George Gemistos Plethon, came to Italy for a church council, and brought with him the notion that all the ancient peoples, pagans as well as Jews and Christians, had possessed divine wisdom. This idea of a *prisca theologia* (ancient theology) was like a spark to the tinder of the Italian humanists, and it set them ransacking the writings of the ancients in search of that wisdom. Zoroaster, Hermes Trismegistus, Orpheus, Pythagoras, and Plato were ranked as sages alongside Moses (who was still believed to have written the first five books of the Old Testament).

Ragon's manuscript does not go much further than these known facts, but the way it puts them is that Plethon introduced the Pythagorean Order into Italy, placing it under the protection of Cosimo de' Medici and Borso d'Este, marquis of Ferrara. Cosimo, we know, was patron of the Platonic Academy of Florence; Borso is not known to have been involved with philosophica matters, but he ruled over an extremely cultured and artistic court and was very independently-minded, so the statement is credible.

Ragon's version of secret history now intersects with that of *The Rule of Four,* for it says that the intitiates of the Pythagorean Order included Cardinal Bessarion and many members of the Roman Academy. They suffered as we have described when it was suppressed, but according to this source, after Pope Paul II's death the Order entered a phase of expansion. Branches were founded in many Italian cities, including Florence, Rome, Perugia, Lucca, Naples, Forli, and Faenza. An academy was opened in Germany, with less success, and one in France which was protected by the kings Louis XII and François I. (I note in passing that François I was also the patron of Leonardo da Vinci, putative member of other secret Orders.)

The Order of Pednosophers consisted of four grades, the first of which was originally open to women and youths as well as to men, and was based on the Greek myth of Deucalion and Pyrrha. These were the only couple left alive after Zeus, like Yahweh in the Hebrew Bible, destroyed the rest of humanity in a worldwide flood. Perhaps, though this is only my speculation, the Pednosophers saw themselves as the bearers of a new and more virtuous strain of humanity. The neophytes (those entering the Order) were expected to be morally irreproachable and to cultivate song, music, and poetry.

A much later promoter of secret societies, the Belgian lawyer Jean Mallinger, claims to have some further knowledge about the Pednosophers. The essential doctrine of the Order, he says, was that of reincarnation—held as we recall by Pythagoras and, in a way, by Plato. The Pednosophers also taught "the Pythagorean conception of a harmonic Universe, whose mathematical symphony has its Ineffable Center in God. Thus Science and Religion are combined in a single cosmic reality." (Mallinger, p. 119) This is a typical trait of esoteric Orders, which accept the findings of science, while seeing no contradiction in them of the truths of religion as they understand them, i.e. in an esoteric way.

Religion, at least since the start of the Christian era, has been a cause for dispute, rivalry, persecution, and even war. This is one reason that the semi-secret Order of Freemasonry forbids its members to discuss religion (or that other bugbear, politics) during its meetings. Ragon indicates that the Pednosophers likewise held themselves aloof from religion and its contradictions:

> ...one might think that the Pednosophers were attached to the paganism that an entirely spiritualized religion [i.e. Christianity] had overturned, but this would be an error. They were too wise and too wary to sacrifice their peace to

those errors that they had all helped to destroy. For them, both religions were equally distant from the truth, which alone deserved their devotion. (Ragon, pp. 70-71)

It sounds from this as though the Order was an essentially philosophic one, giving initiation into a *gnosis* or path to the divine through knowledge that bypassed the dogmas and rituals of religion. Mallinger dwells on the persecutions that such attitudes unleashed:

There were persecutions in Florence; Savonarola is the symbol of the Judeo-Christian reaction; the Holy Office, at the instigation of Cardinal Pamphili, hunted out the initiates everywhere. Fabio Calvo was killed in Rome in 1527; Giordano Bruno was burned alive on February 17, 1600; despite his religious status, Campanella was put in irons: he remained in prison for 27 years and was often tortured; all this to punish him for having revealed a few of the Truths of the more splendid Paganism.
(Mallinger, p. 118)

Mallinger's tale of disaster continues right up to 1761, when two Pythagoreans were arrested in Cologne, accused of spreading heresy.

FROM PEDNOSOPHERS TO TABACCOLOGISTS. Ragon's manuscript states that the only thing that saved the Order from complete extinction was its survival in England, thanks to Sir Thomas Bodley. This statesman, founder of the Bodleian Library in Oxford, had been initiated in Forli in 1554. On his return, he headed an English academy, which gave rise to a brilliant school of Platonists in the later seventeenth century. Then comes a bizarre touch: to avoid attracting attention of the wrong kind, the Order in England and France disguised itself as a club of tobacco-lovers. The members called themselves the "Tabaccologists" or the "Snuff-Takers." All of the centers of the Order were given names of countries from which tobacco came, the headquarters being called "Virginia," Greece being called "Mexico," etc. The past sages of the Order, such as Gemistos Plethon, Bessarion, etc., were concealed under the names of those who had introduced tobacco to Europe: Hernandez, Nicot (from whom we get "nicotine"), Raleigh, Drake, etc.

The Order began to fade in the course of the eighteenth century, and the London headquarters closed down. All its archives, statutes, and rituals were transferred to France, where the Order flourished for a few decades more. But one gets the impression that it was moribund, as no more famous names are associated with it. The last guardian of its archives died in the Napoleonic Wars, leaving his friend, a Monsieur Doussin, as heir to a chest which turned out to contain all the papers of the Pednosophers. Doussin could only understand about half of the initiatic degrees, but in 1806 he bravely started a new school to teach what he could. The Order continued in a hole-in-the-corner way, under the shadow of the French Masonic lodge the "Grand Orient," but by 1848 it had, in Ragon's words, "fallen into a profound sleep." He ends his account with the hope that someone might one day revive it.

Perhaps Jean Mallinger himself took this step. It is rumored in esoteric circles that there is even today an Order based in Paris called "L'Ordre d'Hermès Trismégiste" (Order of Hermes Trismegistus). This Order, which also has a branch in Sweden, claims to descend from the Tabaccologists. Who its members are, and how one contacts them, I have no idea. If Ragon's manuscript tells true, they can pride themselves on a filiation going back through the Academies of Rome and Athens to the Pythagorean Order of the sixth century BC, and even beyond that to ancient

Egypt, where Pythagoras learned his wisdom. As against this, there is the well-known custom of secret societies to pretend that they are descended from some great lineage of the past, such as the Knights Templar, the Priory of Sion, or the Rosicrucians. In the case of an academy, whose object is to teach philosophy, not to flatter people's self-importance by conferring titles and degrees, such filiation is virtually meaningless. But whether this is all the stuff of dreams, and as fantastic as the vaults of Francesco Colonna or Christian Rosenkreutz, the reader once again must decide.

Chapter 5
What does the Hypnerotomachia mean?

According to *The Rule of Four,* Francesco Colonna wrote the *Hypnerotomachia* with the primary objective of transmitting his secret. It was the key to his vault, entrusted to the future in the hope that one day someone might be cunning and fortunate enough to find it. He used an illustrated erotic novel as the hiding-place for this key, knowing that such a work would never fail to attract curious readers. And so it turned out. Long before Colonna's history was decoded, it was the book itself that enthralled all the characters, both the older generation (Patrick Sullivan, Richard Curry, Vincent Taft) and the younger (Bill Stein, Tom Sullivan, Paul Harris).

For most of them, the fascination stopped there. Patrick Sullivan discovered the Belladonna document, which enabled him to solve the authorship question, at least to his own satisfaction. Vincent Taft found his own morbid preoccupations reflected in the novel, and only later became a convert to Sullivan's theory, which he poached from the work of others. Stein, too, was a poacher who never caught his game: he was planning to make Paul's work the hinge-pin of his academic career when he was killed. Richard Curry, discoverer of the Genoese portmaster's diary, must have had suspicions that there was more to it, but he lost the diary. When he retrieved it, he handed the torch on to

Paul. Tom Sullivan himself grew up under the shadow of his father's fascination with the work, but it took Paul Harris to carry his interest further.

Chapter 1 took the *Hypnerotomachia* on its own terms, as most of these characters do, and described what it was. Now we ask what is behind it? What context does it fit into, and whatever does it mean?

THE HARVEST OF A HUNDRED YEARS

The chronology of *The Rule of Four* requires Colonna to have started writing the *Hypnerotomachia* after the Aldine Press had started publishing the classics (see *ROF,* p. 157), hence after 1495. He continued it while also busied with constructing his vault and collecting its contents, not to mention hanging around the docks of Genoa and arranging traps for his accomplices. Writing such a long and complex work would scarcely have been possible in the given time. It is equally unlikely that the architect Terragni could have taken over Book II after Colonna's death in February 1498 and submitted it to Aldus Manutius in time for publication in December 1499. An already painstaking literary style would have been slowed to a snail's pace by using the Rule of Four, which requires the counting of every letter. Finally, drawing the 172 illustrations and having them cut in wood blocks is not the mark of a rushed job.

On the contrary, the book has all the signs of leisurely creation by a single author and the slow maturation of ideas. The fact that a few recondite words were added from sources discovered at the last minute does not contradict this. The classical learning present in such superabundance was the fruit of many years, to say nothing of the knowledge of botany, mineralogy, epigraphy (the reading and writing of classical inscriptions), and architecture. I imagine the *Hypnerotomachia* as having grown by gradual accretions like a coral reef, accumulating ever more fantastic forms and arabesques. There is the passion and the learning of a whole life in it, or rather of a whole century.

Appearing on the symbolic date of December, 1499, the *Hypnerotomachia* harvests the vintage of a hundred years that changed European culture for ever. There had long been a suspicion that the classical civilization of Greece and Rome was superior to the "modern," i.e. what we call the Medieval. The fifteenth century saw that suspicion become certainty when the achievements of the ancients were rediscovered, as in the case of Greek and Roman authors, or looked at with fresh vision, as with ruined buildings and broken sculptures. In Chapter 1 of the present book, Colonna was quoted on the subject of the modern inferiority to the ancients. He bewailed the feeble achievements of his own time, and the poor moral quality of his contemporaries. But he had little reason to feel so pessimistic. His long life overlapped with Brunelleschi, Alberti, and Bramante among architects, with a host of first class painters including the Bellini, Botticelli, and Leonardo, and with equally superb sculptors such as Ghiberti, Donatello, and Michelangelo. All of them strove deliberately to equal, and then to outdo the fabled geniuses of antiquity. Although Colonna as an author is rarely classed in their company, his effort was part of the same impulse. He set out to write an epic fantasy-novel that would stand comparison with anything the ancients could invent.

For this it was necessary to absorb the achievements of the ancients, which he did first by appropriating their language. Colonna took an entire Latin vocabulary, including words almost no one had heard of, and made it his own. Then he had to assimilate the history and learning of the Graeco-Roman world, and thickly pepper his story with references to it. Just as the dissection of *The Rule of Four* in Chapter 6 reveals a network of references that skim the whole of Western culture, so, on a correspondingly larger canvas, the erudition of the *Hypnerotomachia* covers the whole antique world.

These two things—a rich vocabulary and the incessant reference to antiquity—give the surface of the novel its character. It is a bright and coruscating surface, and not, as I have said, a comfortable one to read. Then there is the plot, with its dream-framework, its stories within stories, its long descriptive digressions. An acknowledged model for Colonna's work is Apuleius's *Golden Ass,* one of the few novels to survive from antiquity and the source of much of the *Hypnerotomachia's* vocabulary. But the genre that Colonna is attempting is not really the novel, but the epic.

A PAGAN EPIC

If one turns to compare the *Hypnerotomachia* with some of the epics Colonna is likely to have known, many similarities emerge. I have already mentioned Dante, who likewise included, though in a Christianized cosmos, representative figures and stories from the ancient world. The *Hypnerotomachia* begins just like the *Divine Comedy,* with the narrator lost in a dark wood, and beginning thus, is an invitation to look out for further parallels. One immediately leaps to mind: Poliphilo's journey, like Dante's, falls into a three-part progression, from Hell (the opening chapters, until he escapes from the dragon) through Purgatory (the meeting with Polia and the journey to the sea-shore cemetery) to Paradise (the Island of Venus). Colonna shares with Dante a liking for concentric arrangements: compare the layout of Cytherea with the geography of Dante's Inferno or Purgatory. Both author-narrators have two different guides in the course of their journeys. Dante starts under the guidance of Virgil, then when he comes to Paradise, where the pagan poet is denied entrance, his beloved Beatrice takes over. Poliphilo starts under Polia's tutelage, then both he and Polia become obedient followers of Cupid. Further parallels with Dante could be drawn, but this must suffice here.

Another source of Colonna's ways of thought, coming from the same era, is the romance of chivalry. The search for Polia, as commentators have pointed out, resembles the quest for the beloved woman in the *Romance of the Rose,* an epic poem written in the later 13th century by Guillaume de Loris and Jean de Meun. Likewise, there is a flavor of the Arthurian romances and the quest for the Holy Grail. Poliphilo is very far from being a brave knight, "without fear and without reproach." On the contrary, he is more a passive spectator than a man of action, more coward than hero, and he never pretends to be above the lusts of the flesh. When he is offered the choice of three portals promising worldly glory, spiritual asceticism, or admission to the realm of Venus, his decision would disqualify him from a seat at the Round Table. But it leads him through a wonderland not unlike the Grail kingdom, to which only the most virtuous knights are admitted. In the epic poem of Parsifal, for instance, the Grail castle is staffed by beautiful virgins who enact a strange ceremony, somewhat like the episode of Queen Eleutherylida's court and somewhat like the marriage rite in the Temple of Venus.

We find many more similarities when looking further back, to Greek and Roman epics. In its plethora of catalogues and descriptions, the *Hypnerotomachia* most resembles Homer's *Iliad*: compare the ship-list and the long analysis of the shield of Achilles in Homer with the lists of stones or plants and the architectural descriptions in Colonna. One could draw another parallel with the *Iliad* inasmuch as Poliphilo's story is also one of "strife," though his battle is fought without arms and against no enemy but himself. Comparisons come more readily to mind with Homer's *Odyssey,* an epic whose fairytale atmosphere is closer to that of Colonna's work. Both Poliphilo and Odysseus are on a journey to find their true love, and both are distracted on the way: Odysseus by his affairs with the goddess Circe and the nymph Calypso; Poliphilo by a roving eye for every passing nymph. Both cross the ocean to attain the island of their desire. More particularly, I see a parallel between the courts of Queen Eleutherylida and

King Alcinous. In both of these, the wanderer is exposed to a level of luxury and culture far superior to what he is used to. Both palaces contain automata: watchdogs and light-bearing statues in Homer's version, mechanical fountains in Colonna's. In both courts the hero enjoys a sumptuous feast, followed by a ballet with music that is also a competitive game. But this paradisal episode is only that: he cannot stay there forever.

Another parallel between the *Hypnerotomachia* and the *Odyssey* exists on the structural level: neither story is a straightforward narrative covering a single time-sequence. Homer inserts a parenthesis of several books in which Odysseus recounts his past adventures to the friendly listeners of Alcinous's court. In Book II of the *Hypnerotomachia*, the narratives spoken by Poliphilo and Polia to the nymphs take the reader back in time as they reveal their past histories, and explain how they came to be where they are.

If we wanted to take the parallels further, we might note that when Poliphilo first meets Polia, he takes her for one of the nymphs, and it only later dawns on him that the woman he has been talking to (and feeling greatly attracted to), is in fact his beloved. In Book XIII of the *Odyssey*, Odysseus likewise meets Athena in the guise of a shepherd boy, then sees through her disguise.

This leads us to the obvious remark that both Poliphilo and the Homeric heroes have patrons among the Olympian gods. Athena watches over Odysseus, even descending from Olympus and meeting him on earth, ensuring that against all opposition he will regain his home and throne in Ithaca. Poliphilo's patron is Venus, aided by her son Cupid. He meets her in a theophanic vision, when she appears in her bath at the very center of her isle of Cytherea, and again in heaven, when his soul ascends to beseech her to grant his desire for Polia's love. Moreover, there is a sense of conflict in heaven such as fuels the action of both the *Iliad* and the *Odyssey*. Polia is at first devoted to the goddess Diana, and has consecrated herself to perpetual service as a virgin in her temple. Venus, in granting Poliphilo's desire, is competing with Diana for Polia's allegiance, and with one shaft from Cupid's bow, she wins the mortal over. The corresponding action on earth is where the two lovers are expelled by the furious devotees of Diana and take refuge in Venus's rival temple, where the High Priestess welcomes them.

I leave it to other scholars to seek out the innumerable parallels that may or may not signal actual influences on Colonna, but which indicate what manner of work the *Hypnerotomachia* is. It is a prose epic. The epic genre is usually reserved for poetry, but no poet has paid greater attention to language and to the exact choice of words. Colonna's work contains more than enough of the usual ingredients of an epic, starting with its outsize dimensions. Obviously it has a hero, a quest, a journey, and an overriding sense of tragedy. Beyond that, it includes a theology (showing how God or the gods relate to mankind); a cosmology (showing how the universe is structured); and a cosmogony (explaining how the cosmos came into existence—in this case, through Love). It describes tremendous natural landscapes, and equally monumental works of man. It teaches moral lessons, according to its own scheme of ethics. And it is absolutely unique, just as Homer's epic poems are unique, or Ovid's *Metamorphoses,* Dante's *Divine Comedy*, Milton's *Paradise Lost*, Proust's *A la recherche du temps perdu,* or Tolkien's *Lord of the Rings* (add or subtract as you please). Once read, the imagery and atmosphere of such works remain with one as a permanent possession.

The most remarkable thing about the *Hypnerotomachia,* after its beauty as a book and the wonder of its language, is its paganism. There may be moralizing allegory in it, and an occasional tinge of scholastic philosophy, but the surface is relentlessly and unapologetically pagan. The action takes place in a world inhabited by the ancient gods, goddesses, nymphs, and semi-human beings, just as one finds them in Ovid, for instance.

The scenery is partly that of the ruins of such a world, especially at the beginning of the story and in the episode by the seaside cemetery. There everything is overgrown and many monuments are half-broken, the soil littered with fragments of past glories. Otherwise the ancient monuments of Poliphilo's dream are not only present in their untarnished wholeness, but exceed in size and richness even the descriptions of classical authors. On the isle of Cytherea, nature flourishes in symbiosis with the arts of architecture and garden design. It is a perpetual spring with no beginning and no end. Nor is there any indication of when the place was planned and built: it is a finished and perfect whole, beyond time and mutability. In a word, it is a pagan Elysium. Nothing is lacking for the ultimate in human felicity, here conceived of as the saturation of all the senses and the omnipresence of Love.

The beings of Poliphilo's dream world have no sense of sin, no knowledge of vice. Some of them, like the satyrs or the sea-gods, are rough and boisterous, while others are so pure as to be almost ethereal. Poliphilo's preference is for the ones in between: the nymphs with plump little bodies and elaborate hairdos and footwear. Whatever their status, all the beings in his world are just as they should be. None but Poliphilo seems to have anything to agonize over, or strive for. The violent scenes in Book II take place on earth, and in Polia's dreams (themselves part of Poliphilo's dream), and the whole thrust of their meaning is that Polia should accept the promptings of Eros. Likewise, the sad stories engraved on the tombstones of the seaside cemetery tell of those who have refused love, or whose love has been blighted by circumstance. In the moral scheme of the *Hypnerotomachia,* once love is accepted—and plainly this implies physical, sexual love—Paradise is here and now.

Perhaps this is also the philosophy of *The Rule of Four.* Tom and Katie's relationship carries no suggestion that premarital sex is sinful in itself; the real sins are against loyalty and trust. The strongest bonds of love are those that unite the four male friends, and those between father (or surrogate father) and son. There is also a deep love of place, expressed in the buildings of Princeton, coupled with regret that the characters are so near the point of awakening from the four-year dream that is undergraduate life.

POLIPHILO=LORENZO THE MAGNIFICENT=ROMEO?

Emanuela Kretzulesco has returned to the *Hypnerotomachia* several times in her various books, but her first one, *Les Jardins du songe,* is the foundation of all her writing about it. Still unpublished in English (though a translation does exist), *Les Jardins du songe* is a fine example of the originality and boldness of the independent scholar (Kretzulesco grew up among the priceless Aldine volumes of her family's library in Soragna.)

The first of Kretzulesco's insights is to associate the *Hypnerotomachia* with the love-affair between Lorenzo de' Medici ("The Magnificent") and Lucrezia Donati. It is told that in 1462, when he was sixteen, Lorenzo fell in love with the thirteen-year-old daughter of the aristocratic Donati clan. Beside the fact that she was at first entirely indifferent to him, there was no question of the Donati uniting their family with a middle-class banking family like the Medici. Lucrezia's parents arranged a marriage with another aristocrat, Niccolò Ardinghelli. Since the bride was still so young, after the betrothal Niccolò left to seek his fortune in Middle-Eastern trade. He was away so long that Lucrezia despaired of ever getting married. Whether or not she entered a convent, as Polia did, is not recorded; but in Kretzulesco's reconstruction of Lucrezia's history she did so. It was on the public occasion of her reception into monastic life that Lorenzo saw her again, and again fell madly in love with her. Their subsequent meetings then took place much as described in Book II of the *Hypnerotomachia,* culminating in her cruel rejection of Lorenzo and his falling into a death-like faint.

Like Polia, Lucrezia revived her lover and soon found herself converted to a passionate love for him. With the connivance of a rival convent, the two of them were secretly married. Not long after, Niccolò Ardinghelli returned from his travels, all expectant of his long-awaited wedding. Parental pressure was irresistible, and the nuptials took place with all suitable pomp. Lorenzo was left desolate, but the customs of the time allowed him to make symbolic demonstration of his "courtly" love for the bride, by holding festivals and tournaments in her honor. It was these events that won him the sobriquet of "Il Magnifico." To console him, his father sent him off to Rome, where he became the pupil of Leon Battista Alberti. This brings us back to the first book of the *Hypnerotomachia,* which is based on Alberti's guidance of Lorenzo through the ruins and splendors of Roman antiquity.

The perceptive reader may already have guessed the identity of the next item in Kretzulesco's scheme. The meeting of teenage lovers from hostile families, and their secret marriage, is the subject of Shakespeare's tragedy, *Romeo and Juliet.* To Kretzulesco, the Lorenzo-Lucrezia affair was allegorized in the Italian poem *Giulia e Romeo,* the source of Shakespeare's drama. Thus the *Hypnerotomachia* and *Romeo and Juliet* are twin works, inspired by the same real-life story.

SECRET PHILOSOPHY IN THE GARDEN

The third item in Kretzulesco's complex plot is the *Hypnerotomachia* itself. She reads the work as teaching a body of philosophical truths that were quasi-heretical at the time—hence their concealment in the form of fiction. At the highest metaphysical level, these concern creation itself, and the wonder that things exist at all. "Engendered Being was dreamed by the Uncreated. This caused the differentiation between the One and the Other, which love each other, and are loved with an equal love." This, she says, was the doctrine celebrated in the temple of Fortuna Primigenia at Palestrina, the model for the pyramid-portal of the *Hypnerotomachia*: "Here Being was venerated, as opposed to Nothing." (*Jardins,* p. 94)

This may seem abstract, if not philosophically banal, but it leads to further consequences. "The temple of Palestrina bears witness to a belief common to all the Mediterranean peoples concerning the phenomenon of life, and the fortunate meaning that was given it, at its origin, by the metaphysical Eros... The pilgrim who aspired to mastery of his destiny was impelled to pass his apprenticeship in the Temple of Fortune through nostalgia for a happy state, preceding the mysterious catastrophe that destroyed the earthly paradise and forbade man access to the source of life." (*Jardins,* p. 95) In other words, the created world was originally good, and in a state of mutual love with its Creator, and it is this condition that Poliphilo hopes to regain.

The monuments examined by Poliphilo in the first chapters of the book contain many mythic images, which all relate to the early history of the planet. They refer to the mystery of the first appearance of life in the sea, symbolized by the arising of Venus from the waves; to the great telluric movements that built the continents, symbolized by the battle of the Giants. The winged horse Pegasus teaches him about the journey of the soul after death. "It symbolizes the process of the death of the carnal body and the rebirth of man in eternity. This rebirth is conditioned by an *effort*... Immortality is not given for free: it must be acquired by an effort capable of assuring a sequel to the adventure of the being." (*Jardins*, p. 109)

Kretzulesco makes reference here to the Egyptian and Hermetic doctrines that so enthralled the humanists of the late fifteenth century. The rebirth in question, she says, is in the subtle body, which corresponds in every detail to the physical one: it is the body in which one passes through the experiences described in the *Egyptian Book of the Dead*. The symbol for this in the

Hypnerotomachia is the elephant carrying an obelisk on its back. Inside the great statue, Poliphilo discovers the tombs of a man and a woman, with inscriptions concerning their rebirth. Curiously enough, it was exactly two hundred years after the symbolic date of the *Hypnerotomachia,* on May 1, 1667, that Pope Alexander VII dedicated Bernini's elephant-obelisk on the former site of a temple of Isis. (*Jardins,* pp. 116-117)

Until death, it is important to care for the physical body, and this is the lesson taught by the anatomical colossus whose description was included in Chapter 1. The key to Poliphilo's thought and that of the group of humanists hidden behind this pseudonym is this: "The best way of access to the knowledge of God is that which opens to the human mind the knowledge of nature and its laws. As knowledge becomes perfected, the mind rises to the conception from which they emanate. At the same time, this knowledge of nature permits man to safeguard his life." (*Jardins,* p. 119)

Christian theologians had long stressed the fallen state of man and, with him, of nature, despising the study of the body and the created world. In contrast, Kretzulesco reads the *Hypnerotomachia* as a passionate plea to recognize the essential goodness of nature and of the human body. The physical love that impels Poliphilo is different in degree, but not in kind, from the love that caused the universe to arise in the first place, and which extends through its every atom. Kretzulesco appears in all of her writings as a Christian Neoplatonist, for whom Christ is the manifestation of the same divine Love that Poliphilo celebrates as Venus Urania. Hers is a joyful Christianity that does not harp on original sin and the fallen state of man, but invites the continual presence of redeeming love.

Kretzulesco's fourth topos is the scandal of the Roman Academy's dissolution and the persecution of its members by the Papacy, coupled with the misdeeds of the Borgia Pope Alexander

VI, which I have already treated in Chapter 4. The ending of the *Hypnerotomachia* refers to this by quoting the words of Philomel. As the myth relates, Philomel was raped by king Tereus, who tore out her tongue to prevent her from revealing the fact. She turned into a nightingale, and ever after proclaimed his crime with her song. In Kretzulesco's interpretation, this forced silencing is what happened to the Roman Academy, and the *Hypnerotomachia* is their proclamation.

All of these strands come together in Kretzulesco's fifth subject: the formal gardens of Italy and France in the sixteenth and seventeenth centuries. Her thesis is that, while the doctrines of a positive Christianity were driven underground, their proponents survived. The *Hypnerotomachia* became the bible of a sect without a master, which enrolled many of the great names of the succeeding centuries. As the outer world spiraled down into religious fanaticism and civil war between Christians, these initiates continued to embody the old truths in a place where no heresy⁄hunter would suspect it: in garden design. Kretzulesco guides the reader through the wonderful gardens of Castello, Fontainebleau, Boboli, Bomarzo, Villa d'Este, Collodi, Isola Bella, and Versailles. She shows that they are full of statues, fountains, grottoes, labyrinths, bowers, theaters, obelisks, and topiary formations that seem to be taken straight from Colonna's book, and she reads into each one of them a different philosophical lesson.

I enjoy Kretzulesco's writing, and agree that the allusions to the *Hypnerotomachia* in these gardens cannot be attributable to mere chance. But this is not surprising. The *Hypnerotomachia,* beside its other remarkable qualities, is recognized as a pioneering work of garden design. To any learned person setting out to plan a formal garden on a grand scale, it would have been an obvious inspiration, and a challenge. It is another question whether the use of themes from the *Hypnerotomachia* denotes a transmission of the same philosophical doctrines as she finds in Colonna's book. One has first to accept that these are the real meaning of the *Hypnerotomachia,* and as we will see, there is no consensus on this point.

A JUNGIAN PLUMBS THE DEPTHS

The study of the *Hypnerotomachia* by Linda Fierz-David, published in English in 1950, comes with a foreword by none other than Carl Gustav Jung. He writes there of his early encounter with the *Hypnerotomachia* in its French version of 1600, which interprets it in terms of alchemy. The great psychologist records his puzzlement and frustration with the work, but adds that perhaps it was responsible for his later attraction to alchemical books. He congratulates Fierz-David for making the work at last comprehensible.

Naturally, this interpretation closely follows the principles of Jung's own depth psychology. Fierz-David provides a cursory summary of the story, section by section, interspersed with her commentary. A major theme is the historical context. Poliphilo is a representative of his time, coming at the very end of the Middle Ages and the dawn of a new era in European consciousness. With his fashionable enthusiasm for antiquity, Poliphilo strives to be a modern, that is, a Renaissance man, but in many respects he is still medieval. For example, when he sees the pyramid portal, supposedly the grandest monument of classical antiquity, he invests it with the special quality of Gothic architecture, namely height, and rushes up to its pinnacle as if ascending a cathedral spire. Heaven for him, though not for the ancients, is still Above. But looking to the future, Poliphilo represents the man who is beginning to feel himself not simply as filling the place assigned him in society, but as an individual with a personal destiny. Fierz-David compares him on the one hand to the Dante of the *Divine Comedy,* with which she sees many parallels and even borrowings, and on the other to the Faust of Goethe's dramas. Despite the difference in time-periods, she sees Poliphilo as having more in common with Faust than with Dante.

Fierz-David's interpretation hinges on two main themes of Jungian psychology: the existence of four functions in the human being, and that of the unconscious correlative of the opposite sex. In men, this is called the anima; in women, the animus. Much of her analysis of Poliphilo has to do with the predicament of a typically learned man of his time—and of ours—who lives in his head and deals with his problems through the functions of thinking and intuition. He falls into difficulties when the other two functions of feeling and sensation make demands on him. They bring about exaggerated and even absurd reactions, such as Poliphilo shows throughout his love-quest. For example, he has a deep and scholarly interest in architecture and in the remnants of classical antiquity, but the moment he sees a nymph, his body takes charge and he is obsessed with sensual desire.

In a more complex example, Fierz-David interprets the four triumphal processions as representing the four functions and their corresponding elements of Earth (Europa), Air (Leda), Fire (Danaë), and Water (Semele). At the sight of the fourth chariot, the one bearing the vine of Dionysus, Poliphilo feels disquiet and repulsion, which betrays this as the symbol of his inferior function. It awakens in him the fear of madness, yet it is this very function that can open the way of initiation to him. The symbols on the sides of the Dionysian chariot make this plain: they show the transformation of nymphs into trees, symbolizing the stages of alchemy, and the hermaphrodite Bacchus with two serpents, symbolizing the One that underlies the whole alchemical process.

Polia is naturally the personification of Poliphilo's anima. He does not regard her as a person in her own right, but sees her purely through the mists of his own obsessions. When he speaks or writes to her, it is always about himself, how he feels, how he suffers. In short, he makes a fool of himself, and, in the endless tirades of Book II, a bore. Polia, on the contrary, comes alive in

Book II, having been up to then merely a figure in Poliphilo's besotted imagination. In contrast to him, she tells her story with cool objectivity, describing happy and tragic events with the same dispassion. She appears not as goddess on a pedestal, but as a rather ordinary and not very kindly young woman. At the same time, she deflates the lofty claims of Poliphilo the Renaissance humanist, and shows him to himself in all his ordinariness. They are now two human beings, facing the world without illusions.

The ingredients that went into this process of trans-formation include the Renaissance attitude to antiquity, alchemy, and the Medieval concept of courtly love. Through his immersion in antiquity, Poliphilo learns a new attitude towards the body and its desires; he is no longer ashamed of them, as dogmatic Christianity has taught him to be. This transposes itself into a new objective attitude towards the world in general: it is to be taken as it is, not as clothed by dogma and superstition. Obviously this points forward to the scientific attitude that would appear a hundred years later.

Alchemy is too complicated and obscure a subject to be entered on here. It is enough to say that Fierz-David sees the *Hypnerotomachia* as rich in alchemical symbolism, especially the symbolism of numbers which is the most primordial element in alchemy. This is especially the case when she treats the mysterious three-sided obelisk, standing on its circular plinth and square base. She interprets the Temple of Venus Physizoa as an alchemical vessel in which the *hieros gamos,* the sacred marriage and fusion of opposites, takes place.

As for courtly love, that is the natural form of expression for a writer coming at the end of the Middle Ages. The court of Queen Eleutherylida, especially, is a perfect fantasy of the medieval court, with its extreme observance of hierarchy and ritual behavior. In courtly love, the love of a woman is supposed to be a spur for higher things: in Dante's case, for spiritual ascent; in the case of poets like Petrarch, as a Muse to inspire artistic achievement. Likewise in the *Hypnerotomachia* it is possible to read the story as an ascent from physical to sublimated love. But to Fierz-David, there is an incompleteness in the story, for Poliphilo never achieves what a Jungian could consider the integration of the personality. Like the ideal courtly lover, he attains his beloved only in the higher realm of Venus, leaving behind the earth and that inconvenient, unintegrated fourth function. His attainment is a beautiful illusion—a dream.

THE PURE AIR OF NEOPLATONISM

The palm for the deepest penetration of the *Hypnerotomachia* should be awarded to Marco Ariani and Mino Gabriele, for their achievement in translating the work into modern Italian, supplying it with extensive notes and introductory essays. Not only does this make a volume of more than 1000 pages, but it accompanies a facsimile, in reduced size, of the original work. Gabriele signs the essay on "The Voyage of the Soul," Ariani "The Philosophical Dream," both written from a Neoplatonic perspective.

Neoplatonism is the name given, after the fact, to the schools of philosophers that took Plato as their master. After Plato's death in 347 B.C., his teachings were continued in the Athenian Academy which he had founded, but they suffered an eclipse as the rival schools of Stoicism and Epicureanism took the field. Only around the time of Christ did Platonism begin its return to prominence, especially in the intellectual melting pot of Alexandria. By that time, Plato's philosophy had become blended with the practices of magic and theurgy (the science of evoking the gods), and with the mystery-religions of Egypt and the Near East that promised salvation to their initiates.

The Neoplatonic philosophers of the succeeding centuries ranged from the austere Plotinus, with his intricate analyses of the soul and the spiritual universe, to the mystagogue Iamblichus, fascinated with oriental customs and Egyptian rites. But they all shared one of the fundamental tenets of Plato's teaching: that the material world is an inferior copy of a higher world. The latter is sometimes called the World of Forms, sometimes that of Ideas, and to attain it is held out as the most desirable destiny of the human being. Just as the universe consists of different levels of being, material and spiritual, so do we consist of body and soul. But we also possess higher elements still, notably what the Neoplatonists call Intellect. This is not to be confused with simple intelligence, but is a faculty of direct perception through which we are able to know the Forms.

Obviously this is a philosophy that cannot be explained in a couple of paragraphs, but this sketch must suffice as an introduction to Ariani and Gabrieli's reading of the *Hypnerotomachia*.

According to this, the *Hypnerotomachia* tells of the voyage of the soul freed from the body. In this condition, the soul is pulled in two opposite directions. Its earthly desires and illusions hold it down, while its attraction to immortal virtues and intelligence draws it upwards. In Poliphilo's case, the voyage takes him from blind, libidinous desire to the sublime, initiatic light of the celestial Venus, mother and lover of all.

Gabriele emphasizes the fact that at the beginning of his journey, already in a dream, Poliphilo falls asleep again. He likens this dreaming within a dream to the ancient practice of incubation: a person would spend the night in a temple with the intention of meeting a god or goddess in the dream state. True to type, Poliphilo first encounters "phantasms": architecture and sculptures inflated to impossible proportions, which represent the physical body in which the soul is still partially imprisoned.

The fear that invariably accompanies the separation of the soul from the body is represented by the dragon, which chases

Poliphilo through the labyrinthine passages until he bursts out into the light of a new world. He is then led by five nymphs whose names refer to the five senses, representing his transition from the physical to the spiritual senses. They bring him to the realm of Eleutherylida, an image of the natural world which he can now perceive in its true form as the gift of Mother Nature. Here he is first taught the chief and repeated lesson of the *Hypnerotomachia*: *"Festina lente,"* hasten slowly, if one is to achieve one's goal.

The Neoplatonic interpretation of the work emphasizes an episode that I have not yet mentioned. In Eleutherylida's secret garden, Poliphilo beholds a three-faced obelisk standing on a circular and square base. Its numerical symbolism is explained to him in complex philosophical terms, evidently referring to the deepest metaphysical teachings of Platonism. In short, it describes how the One becomes a Trinity, and thereby generates the entire cosmos. Ariani makes the point that once he has seen this monument, Poliphilo hurries on past it. It signifies that Colonna has given us a hint of the ultimate philosophical mysteries, but that Poliphilo is on a different quest. He is not seeking union with the One, like Plotinus or certain Christian mystics, but an initiation into the mysteries of the Celestial Venus, i.e. the higher love that engenders and permeates the universe.

After he has passed the three portals, Poliphilo learns further lessons about the nature of love. On the one hand, he beholds the triumphal processions depicting the loves of Zeus, proclaiming the power of Cupid over even the gods. On the other, he sees a depiction of Hell, in which those who have refused love's dominion are tormented in an endless round between fire and ice. Through all of this, Poliphilo depicts himself mercilessly as a "philosophic ass" (the reference is to Apuleius's *The Golden Ass)*, filled with sensuality, curiosity, and lust. But it is these very qualities that press him onwards to discover the ever more ethereal and light-filled realms of his dream.

When Poliphilo and Polia cross the sea to the island of Cytherea, they enter a place of perfectly geometrical construction that symbolizes the heavens. Here it is the cosmogenic Eros, the love that keeps all the planets and stars in harmonious motion, that manifests through gardens, architecture, triumphs, and mythological beings. As the lovers progress from the shore of the circular island to its center, everything becomes increasingly rich and luminous, and nature and art blend indistinguishably. At the climax of Book I, they reach the axis of the world in the form of Venus's bath, and behold her naked. But Gabriele says that even here, the lovers are still in the realm of the lower love. Immediately after, they are shown the tomb of Adonis, which commemorates Venus's own subjection to earthly desire. Only in Book II, which returns to the real world, do Poliphilo and Polia achieve the vision of Venus Urania, the celestial Venus.

As Book II begins, the lovers are poles apart: Poliphilo is burning with sexual desire, as he has been for the whole of Book I, while Polia is frigidly indifferent to him, and to love in general. They both need to attain the "golden mean." As in Book I, they first go through a ceremony in Venus's temple, then they have an epiphany of the goddess herself. But the epiphany in Book II is not just an objective vision, but a face-to-face meeting; Venus is not seen in her bath with her lover Mars, but alone in the celestial realm. This experience brings the two lovers to a point of equilibrium at which true love can be realized.

Ariani and Gabriele comment on how, unlike Plato, Colonna does not see the higher love as supplanting the lower one, but as coexisting with it. In this, they say, lies his true originality as a philosopher.

Although these summaries give only a glimpse of the various interpretations, they do show that there is much more to the *Hypnerotomachia* than any of the characters in *The Rule of Four* have suspected. Five hundred years after its appearance, it is still a lure to scholars and a delight to readers at every philosophical level. In fact, it is thanks to *The Rule of Four* that it has found a new audience, and its outlandish name, if only people can pronounce it, is becoming a household word.

Chapter 6
The Rule of Four Dissected: Annotations of Names, Places, Literary Quotations, etc.

This chapter lays bare the nerves and veins which run beneath the surface of the story and give it much of its life and depth. *The Rule of Four* far exceeds in its erudition the usual mystery novel, even the ones that pretend to unveil historical enigmas. It is a mine of references and allusions to literature, both English and foreign, to history, philosophy, and the fine arts.

In 1994, Princeton inaugurated a year-long course, "Introduction to Western Culture," returning to the traditional idea of such studies as the foundation for a liberal arts education. The four undergraduates of *The Rule of Four,* if they were fortunate enough to take that course, could have acquired much of the learning they display in the story, and, equally importantly, the knowledge of where to go for more. While most of these references turn out to be genuine, a few of them, as dictated by the plot or the authors' whim, are spurious.

ROF = *The Rule of Four,* first U.S. edition. *HP* = *Hypnerotomachia Poliphili,* pagination as in the English translation of 1999, which is virtually identical to that of Ariani and Gabriele's facsimile edition (the original of 1499 is not paginated in modern style). For other abbreviated source-references, see the Bibliography at the end of this book.

The Dust-Jacket. This is a clever designer's montage that should not deceive anyone into thinking that it depicts an original copy of the *Hypnerotomachia.* The illustration from *HP*, p. 401 (our Illustration 13) has been fitted into one of the panels of the spine of a vellum-bound book, in the place where the title would normally appear. The faint background designs on the dust-jacket are also a collage, using the initial letter "P" from the first chapter and the schematic garden plan from *HP*, p. 317, with some illegible text.

Page [vii] "Gentle reader, hear Poliphilo tell of his dreams"

This is the beginning of one of at least six prefatory essays or elegies that precede the *Hypnerotomachia* proper. The first is Leonardo Grassi's dedication, written in Latin prose. The second, third (this one), and sixth are in Latin verse; the fourth, in Italian prose; the fifth, in Italian verse. Taken together, they cover both the classical and the "vulgar" language, each in both its forms of prose and verse. It is not known whether they were written by the author, or by those in charge of the publication.

The ellipsis in the passage as quoted indicates the omission of six lines, which refer to the architectural details that have little relevance in *The Rule of Four,* but were of obsessive interest to Colonna:

> Here are pyramids, baths and vast colossi,
>> And the ancient form of obelisks appears.
> A novel pedestal shines forth, and various columns
>> With arch, zophorus, epistyle,
> Capital and beam, the square symmetry
>> Of the cornice, and all that makes a splendid roof.

Page 1. "A church named San Lorenzo"

The messengers Rodrigo and Donato meet their due deserts in the basilica of San Lorenzo fuori le Mura (Saint Lawrence outside the walls), Rome. Its location is shown on the map, *ROF* p. 174, and its six-columned portico is mentioned on *ROF* p. 3.

2. "A starry sky was still painted on the ceiling"
This was because Michelangelo (1475-1564) had not yet painted the Sistine Chapel ceiling with his famous scenes of the Creation, Prophets, Sybils, etc.

3. "lo'mperador del doloroso regno"
"The emperor of the dolorous realm," i.e. Satan as emperor of Hell or the Inferno, as described in Dante's *Divine Comedy*, *Inferno* xxxiv, 28. The "greatest sinners" chewed forever in Satan's jaws are Brutus and Cassius (assassins of Julius Caesar, hence betrayers of the Empire) and Judas Iscariot (betrayer of Christ).

4. "the serpent's teeth that Cadmus sowed"
Cadmus, while searching for his sister Europa, slew a serpent or dragon, and was advised by Athena to sow its teeth in the ground. They sprouted and turned into warriors, who then attacked and killed each other until all were dead. Cadmus founded a city on the spot, which later became Thebes. The story is told in Ovid, *Metamorphoses,* Book 3.

5. "The night of Good Friday has fallen"
The "present day" story of *The Rule of Four* begins in 1999, when Good Friday fell on April 2nd.

6. "instead of Daisy Buchanan we're watching Holly Golightly"
Daisy is the heroine of *The Great Gatsby* by F. Scott Fitzgerald. Holly Golightly is the heroine of *Breakfast at Tiffany's* by Truman Capote (film, with Audrey Hepburn, 1961).

"the emperor was actually taller"
According to Hilaire Belloc, *Napoleon*, 1932, p. 86, Napoleon was 5'7" in English measure. Comparison of foot measures is complicated by the fact that before metrication the French used several different "feet."

7. "I'm sure Frankenstein scholarship will forever be the same"
Frankenstein, or the Modern Prometheus (1813), novel by Mary Wollstonecraft Shelley (1797-1851) about Dr. Frankenstein and the (unnamed) human monster he created.

"a labyrinthine name I can pronounce"

As said in Chapter 1, the most likely pronunciation is "HIP⁄ne⁄RO⁄to⁄MA⁄kia PO⁄li⁄FEE⁄li," and the protagonists are called PO⁄li⁄FEE⁄lo and Po⁄LEE⁄a. Some people say Po⁄LI⁄fi⁄lo and POH⁄li⁄a, but a scholar like Patrick Sullivan would surely have followed the Italian pronunciation rule and stressed the penultimate syllables.

8. "Tobias Smollett. He was a surgeon"

Tobias Smollett (1721⁄1771), novelist, trained and practiced as a surgeon, and graduated M.D. from the University of Aberdeen in 1750.

15. "Arcangelo Corelli Sullivan"

Arcangelo Corelli (1653⁄1713), Italian composer of instrumental music, was influential on Handel, Vivaldi, and J. S. Bach. It is unlikely that Haydn or Mozart paid much attention to his works, of which they would have known a few violin sonatas, at most.

19. "lasciate ogne speranza"

The inscription that Dante, guided by Virgil, reads on the gates of Hell. Dante, *Inferno,* iii, 9.

22. "Something Melvillian"

Reference is to the whale⁄lore in *Moby Dick,* the novel by Herman Melville (1819⁄1891) reluctantly read by all English majors.

"Like Pinocchio"

In *Pinocchio,* the novel (1883) by Carlo Collodi (1826⁄1890), the puppet⁄hero is swallowed by a whale, inside which he finds his maker Gepetto and helps the two of them to safety.

37. "The Hypnerotomachia Poliphili"

See the separate chapters of this book for analysis of its contents, meaning, and debates about its author's identity.

"Marcel Proust, who wrote the world's longest book"

The book in question is the six⁄volume novel *A la recherche du temps perdu* (In search of lost time) by Marcel Proust (1871⁄1922). Tom Sullivan refers to the incident of the narrator's tasting a madeleine (a kind of cake) dipped in herb tea, whereupon, recalling a similar incident in his youth, he suddenly becomes aware of the subtle link between past and present.

38. "Handel's 'Hallelujah Chorus'"

The decision of the Trustees to admit women to Princeton in April, 1969 was celebrated with a broadcast of the "Hallelujah Chorus" from Handel's *Messiah*. (*A Princeton Companion,* p. 530).

"What is Enlightenment?"

An essay (1784) by Immanuel Kant (1724-1804), which begins: "Enlightenment is man's emergence from his self-immured immaturity."

39. "The Gutenberg Bible"

Otherwise known as the "42-line Bible": the first book printed from movable type, using the process perfected by Johann Gutenberg in Mainz, and completed by 1455.

40. "He led me on a tour of the city's fountains"

The three fountains mentioned were the work of the sculptor and architect Gian Lorenzo Bernini (1598-1680). The Barcaccia (1627-29) is the fountain in the shape of a boat in Piazza di Spagna, at the foot of the Spanish Steps. The Fontana del Tritone (1642) in Piazza Barberini has its basin supported by a triton or merman. The Fontana dei Quattro Fiumi (Fountain of the four rivers, 1648-51) in Piazza Navona is Bernini's largest, and it supports an Egyptian obelisk. Incidentally, another of Bernini's Roman landmarks, the elephant with an obelisk upon its back in Piazza della Minerva, is derived from an illustration on p. 38 of the *Hypnerotomachia*.

41. "in broken Tuscan"

The Tuscan dialect was the form of Italian spoken in Tuscany (the region north of Rome including Florence, Siena, and Pisa). Thanks to a distinguished line of Tuscan poets, it became standard Italian, as distinct from the dialects of Latium (the region around Rome), Liguria (around Genoa), and the Veneto (around Venice). The fact that the *Hypnerotomachia* leans towards the latter dialect is one of the strongest arguments against a Roman authorship.

42. "The Belladonna Document"

A wholly fictitious invention. The account of the *Hypnerotomachia* and the candidates for its authorship on *ROF,* pp. 42-43 is loosely accurate, but see Chapter 3 for a thorough treatment of this matter.

44. "Merton's Seven Storey Mountain"

Thomas Merton (1915-1968), American Trappist monk, author of works popularizing Christian mysticism.

"I find great comfort in Auden"

Wystan Hugh Auden, (1907-1973), English poet, known for his war-poems and his Christian pessimism.

45. "The Count of Monte Cristo"

Novel (1845) by Alexandre Dumas *Père* (1802-1870). It tells of a man's quest for revenge on those responsible for his unjust imprisonment.

"Dickens had rewritten Great Expectations"

Charles Dickens (1812-1870) changed the ending of *Great Expectations* between its appearance in magazine installments and its final form as a novel (1861). His fellow novelist Bulwer-Lytton persuaded him that Pip, the hero, deserved a happy ending.

46. "The Rome of Raphael"

The titles of Patrick Sullivan's writings, like the character himself, are fictitious but plausible. *The Rome of Raphael* refers to the painter and architect Raphael Sanzio (1483-1520), born in Urbino but mostly active in Rome. *Ficino and the Rebirth of Plato* concerns the Florentine philosopher Marsilio Ficino (1433-1499), who made the first Latin translation of Plato's works under Medici patronage. *The Men of Santa Croce* is an intriguing title. In the context, it probably refers to the humanists who frequented the Florentine church of Santa Croce in the fifteenth century, including Leon Battista Alberti and Leonardo Bruni. Both are buried there. It might also include the many artists who decorated the walls of the church, including Giotto and Taddeo Gaddi; Brunelleschi, the architect of its Pazzi Chapel, one of the first masterpieces of Renaissance style; and the other eminent persons buried there, who include the astronomer Galileo and (from a much later period) the composer Rossini. The article "The *Hypnerotomachia Poliphili* and the Hieroglyphics of Horapollo" refers to the work by a Greek writer of about the fifth century that purported to explain Egyptian hieroglyphs. It is further treated, with some contempt, on *ROF,* p. 236. "The Breeches-Maker" is an in-joke for art-historians, for he can only be Michelangelo's pupil Daniele da Volterra (1509-1566). He was thus nicknamed because at the Pope's insistence he painted loincloths on the nude figures of Michelangelo's *Last Judgment* in the Sistine Chapel. For an allusion to this, see *ROF,* p. 63. The journals cited are a mixture of real ones (*Renaissance Quarterly, Journal of Interdisciplinary History*) and invented ones (*Journal of Medical History, Bulletin of the American Renaissance Society*).

47. "Please, sir, I want some more"

Oliver Twist, in Charles Dickens's novel of the same name, makes the mistake of asking Mr. Bumble, the beadle in charge of his orphanage, for a second helping.

48. "Strunk and White"

The book on Paul's desk must be *The Elements of Style*, by William Strunk and E.B. White, first published 1949 with many later editions. It is a standard authority for writing and stylistic matters in American universities.

52. "Where Princeton keeps its copy"

According to the National Union Catalogue, Princeton University Library does own a copy of the *Hypnerotomachia.*

54. "I've never heard of William Caxton in my life"

William Caxton (c. 1422-1491) was the most important early English printer, whose publications included the *Canterbury Tales* of Geoffrey Chaucer (c. 1343-1400).

"Aldus's Letters of Saint Catherine"

The letters of Saint Catherine of Siena, published by Aldus in 1500 as *Epistolae devotissime de Sancta Catherina da Siena.*

"Not, as generally believed, the first use of italics"

Among the achievements of Aldus Manutius the Elder (1449-1515) was the design of an italic type fount based on humanistic handwriting. It was first used a year later, in Aldus's octavo edition of Virgil, 1501, and remained standard in the pocket editions of the Aldine Press. Italics do not occur in the *Hypnerotomachia.*

"something roughly the size of a brick"

This is the Genoese portmaster's diary. Like the Belladonna Document, it and its contents are wholly fictitious.

57. *"Our weakness at Fornovo. The old defeat at Portofino."*

The tactless reference is to two defeats. The Venetian League was narrowly defeated by the French at the Battle of Fornovo, 1495, and the Venetian fleet by the Genoese at Portofino, 1432.

58. *"Weh! Steck ich in dem Kerker noch?"*

"Woe! Am I still stuck in this cell, damned musty hole-in-the-wall, where even the precious daylight breaks through dark-stained panes!" From the opening speech of Johann Wolfgang von Goethe's *Faust,* before the entrance of Mephistopheles.

60. *"Leviathan"*

Philosophical treatise on government by Thomas Hobbes (1588-1679). The quotation is from chapter 12, and refers to the state of mankind when there is no governance by a common power, and life degenerates into the "war of all against all."

61. *"Madness in great ones must not unwatched go"*

This is the last line of Act III, Scene 1, of Shakespeare's

62. *"The parts of the Hypnerotomachia that fascinated him"*

A donkey is sacrificed at the altar of Priapus (*HP,* p. 194). During the marriage ceremony of Poliphilo and Polia in the Temple of Venus, a pair of white male swans and a pair of white turtle-doves have their throats cut with a sacrificial knife (*HP,* pp. 226, 231).

Apart from these incidents, which were standard religious practice in the ancient world, the work is neither bloody nor violent.

69. "sorority girl who called him Tiger"

The choice of the Hallowe'en colors of orange and black as the college colors seems to have been responsible for the adoption of the tiger, rather than the heraldic lion, as the Princeton mascot. (*A Princeton Companion,* p. 470.)

"alluding not to Princeton but to Blake"

The allusion is to *The Tyger,* a poem from *Songs of Experience* by William Blake (1757-1827).

70. "where Einstein had worked"

Alfred Einstein (1879-1955) was a Fellow of the Institute for Advanced Study from 1933 until his death.

"Skinner's Auction House in Boston"

This is a real institution, founded in the 1960s.

73. "performing Tom Stoppard's Arcadia"

There follow authentic quotations from *Arcadia* (1993) by Tom Stoppard (born 1937). This is an appropriate allusion, for *The Rule of Four* rivals Stoppard's play in its need for annotation, as well as emulating its plot. For instance, both novel and play take place in two time frames, that of the present day involving characters who are trying to understand what happened in the historical one. Both hinge on an identification, or misidentification, of a document by a historical figure (here Colonna, there Byron). And they both end in fire.

76. "Joseph Selling Wheat to the People"

These are genuine paintings. Bartholomeus Breenbergh (1598/1600-1657), *Joseph Distributing Corn in Egypt,* is in the Barber Institute of Fine Arts, Birmingham. Franz Maulbertsch (1724-1796), *Joseph and His Brothers,* is in the Museum of Fine Arts, Budapest. Incidentally, it does not show an obelisk, whereas Breenbergh's painting does. Jacopo Pontormo (1494-1557), *Joseph in Egypt,* belongs to the National Gallery, London.

The twin paintings by Andrea del Sarto (1486–1530), *Stories of Joseph*, are in the Pitti Palace, Florence.

"Have you read Browning's poem on Andrea del Sarto?"

The quotation is from *Andrea del Sarto* by Robert Browning (1812–1889), lines 69–71. See also the Authors' Note, *ROF,* p. 369.

82. "a framed reproduction of the Hypnerotomachia's title page"

This seems an unlikely image for display, since the title page consists not of a picture but only of a few lines of print (see Chapter 1 of this book).

85. "leafing through his copy of Braudel"

Fernand Braudel, *The Mediterranean and the Mediterranean World in the Age of Philip II*, 1949.

92. "stitched together from the ruins of buildings"

This is hard to imagine in rational terms, because the kind of information supposedly given by Colonna is not present. The idea may have been suggested by the woodcut of ruins on page 238 of the *Hypnerotomachia*.

96. "A rearrangement of the letters in 'doppelganger'"

From German *Doppelgänger*, a double or spook resembling oneself, the meeting of which is supposed to presage death. Goethe famously encountered his own Doppelgänger (and lived long afterwards).

97. "Leonardo wrote that a painter should begin every canvas"

Perhaps based on the passage in *The Practice of Painting* by Leonardo da Vinci (1452–1519), III, 555 in the Richter edition of Leonardo's writings.

103. "the affluence of Exeter"

Gil Rankin was (predictably) educated at Phillips Academy, Exeter, New Hampshire, an exclusive private school founded by Dr. John Phillips in 1781.

107. "Jonathan Edwards"

See the Authors' Note, *ROF,* p. 370.

109. "Saint Denis"

Vincent Taft misrepresents this and other medieval martyrdom legends by relating them as established fact, while they are all more or less apocryphal. The history of Saint Denis, a patron saint of France, is irrevocably muddled by the medieval confusion of three separate people: Saint Paul's companion Denis or Dionysus; a French bishop, possibly martyred c. 250; and a 6th-century mystical author, now called Pseudo-Dionysus the Areopagite.

"*Saint Quentin*"

Subject of a much-embellished story of a Roman missionary to Gaul. Jacob Jordaens (1593-1678) painted many saints, but I cannot find mention of this one in his inventory of works.

"*Saint Lawrence*"

A popular patron saint of uncertain date, who most modern scholars think was beheaded, not roasted. Thus his legendary saying: "Turn me over: I'm done enough on that side" must be dismissed as apocryphal.

110. "*Saint Erasmus*"

Bishop of Formiae in Campania, martyred under the Emperor Diocletian, c. 303.

"*Saint Peter*"

Supposedly martyred in Rome c. 64 AD. Michelangelo's fresco painting of *The Crucifixion of Saint Peter* (painted 1545-1550) is in the Pauline Chapel of the Vatican.

118. "*Hebrew, Arabic, and Chaldean*"

According to "Philologos," a columnist for the *New York Jewish Forward*, June 25 and July 2, 2004, the Hebrew inscriptions in the *Hypnerotomachia* are correct, indeed so fluent that they were probably supplied by a rabbi. Moreover, the pious translator has avoided the charge of polytheism by replacing Venus's title "The Mother of Love," with the impersonal "The nourishment of love." The Arabic texts, in contrast, are so garbled that they were probably compiled from a dictionary. In addition, the left and right-hand inscriptions are reversed. (Thanks to John Patrick Deveney for alerting me to this learned source.)

121. *"A criminal convicted of high treason"*

Prof. Taft manages to include both the meanings assigned by the *Oxford English Dictionary* to the term "drawn," when used of criminals: dragging to the scaffold before hanging, and disemboweling afterwards.

122. *"the opening canto of Dante's 'Inferno'"*

Lines 41-49 introduce in turn a leopard, a lion, and a wolf. Much has been written about their intended symbolism.

"the sixth verse of Jeremiah"

Jeremiah 5:6 promises that disobedient Israel will be assaulted by a lion from the forest, a wolf from the desert, and a leopard.

"But here the Hypnerotomachia diverges"

Indeed it does. Colonna's narrative includes a regular zoo, with a pack of hounds, lions, wolves, eagles, kites, and vultures (*HP* p. 402), while his illustration (p. 403) adds a dragon. It is true that he does not include a leopard.

139. *"Mary Shelley, who was nineteen"*

See note to p. 7. She lost a premature infant in March, 1815, and started writing *Frankenstein* in June, 1816. Her mother died a few days after her birth on August 30, 1797.

141. *"indebted to a book called Cornucopiae"*

Colonna's use of words that first appeared in Perotti's dictionary of this name is one of the main pieces of evidence for the date of the *Hypnerotomachia*'s composition.

143. *"Every letter in the Hebrew alphabet has a number"*

This is the basis of the Kabbalistic reading of the Hebrew scriptures, in which words and phrases are reduced to significant numbers. The same applies to the Greek alphabet, and to the corresponding reading of hidden meanings into the original Greek text of the New Testament, where the process is called "gematria."

"lectures on the Sephirothic correspondences"

The ten Sephiroth are an important element of Kabbalistic philosophy. They represent ten powers of God, and are generally drawn in the form of a tree. The theory of correspondences holds that the various levels of reality, such as the spiritual, the planetary, and the material worlds, are all structured similarly, so that one corresponds to the other. In Kabbalism, each world reflects the structure of the Sephirothic tree. Paul is probably right, though: it doesn't seem to relate to Colonna.

"I looked up every ancient labyrinth I knew"

The Egyptian labyrinth, according to Herodotus, *Histories,* II, 148, contained the tombs of the sacred crocodiles. The labyrinths of Lemnos (an island in the Aegean Sea) and Clusium (in Italy) are mentioned by Pliny the Elder, *Natural History,* XXXVI, xix, 86/93. The Cretan labyrinth is the most famous: built by the legendary King Minos, it housed the Minotaur who was slain by Theseus, aided by Princess Ariadne. Probably the only true labyrinths were those of Egypt and Crete, the term then being transferred to any underground temple or tomb/complex.

"there were four different labyrinths in the Hypnerotomachia"

The one in a temple (*HP,* pp. 247/248) leads Poliphilo to contemplate a painting of Hades and the fate of souls. The one underground comes early in the book (*HP,* pp. 62/67), where in the "blind entrails and winding channels of the dark caverns," Poliphilo is pursued by a dragon. The water/labyrinth, situated in a garden, is shown to Poliphilo (*HP,* pp. 124/127) as a moral lesson which he ignores, preferring follow Love rather than Logic. The "one in a garden" perhaps refers to the series of knot/gardens enclosed by hedges on the Island of Cytherea (*HP,* pp. 316/325).

144. *"My only recourse was to beg the pity of Cretan Ariadne"*

Poliphilo does so when lost in the forest at the beginning of his journey (*HP,* p. 15). Ariadne provided the thread that enabled her lover Theseus to enter the Cretan Labyrinth, kill the Minotaur, and escape.

146. *"a famous humanist who used the eye as his symbol"*

Alberti's symbol appears on the reverse of his portrait medal (c.1446/1450) by Matteo de' Pasti. It shows an eye with an eagle's wing attached above, and seven rays beneath it. At the corners are lines reminiscent of a conventionalized thunderbolt. The motto that accompanies it, QVID TVM, ("what next") is as enigmatic as the emblem itself.

147. "I started hitting Vitruvian terms"

The *Hypnerotomachia*'s architectural portions draw largely on the first century Roman architect Vitruvius's treatise *De Architectura*.

"Horns, as early as Artemidorus"

This refers to *Oneirocritica*, a book on how to interpret dreams by the second century Greek writer Artemidorus Daldianus. The traditional connection of horns with cuckoldry is not found in that book, however: it is much later. Curiously, horns were originally a sign of honor (e.g. as found adorning helmets, especially in German heraldry), and to *lose* them was dishonorable (cf. Italian *scornato* = de/horned, disgraced). By Shakespeare's time, the meaning was reversed.

148. "and claims that the name of the Cushite"

The claim that Moses married an Ethiopian woman is made in Josephus's *Jewish Antiquities,* II, 10, 252.

150. "I found the answer in Hartt's History"

Frederick Hartt, *History of Renaissance Art*, 1970 and later editions: a standard art/historical textbook.

151. "Michelangelo's statue of Moses"

Carved in 1516 for the tomb of Pope Julius II, in the church of San Pietro in Vinculis, Rome.

"When Saint Jerome translated the Old Testament"

Exodus 34:35 reads in Saint Jerome's version (the Vulgate): "videbant faciem egredientis Mosi esse cornutam," i.e. "They saw that Moses' face, as he came out, was horned." This has been the cause of many strange/looking representations of Moses in sculpture and painting.

153. "He wrote Curious George"

The popular children's book about a monkey was written and illustrated in 1941 by Hans Augusto and Margret Rey.

"taking to Pynchon and DeLillo"

American novelists Thomas Pynchon (b. 1937) and Don DeLillo (b. 1936)

157. *"If it is true, what Pico said"*

Pico della Mirandola (1463–1494), in his *Oration on the Dignity of Man*, a clarion cry of Renaissance humanism that was silenced by Savonarola and his kind.

"as Hermes Trismegistus claimed"

In *Asclepius,* 6a, a Latin dialogue attributed to the apocryphal Egyptian sage Hermes Trismegistus or "Thrice–Greatest Hermes." The Hermetic writings, first translated into Latin by Ficino, were a blend of genuine Egyptian teachings with Neoplatonism. Their philosophy underlay much of Renaissance alchemy and magic.

158. *"Corelli's Christmas Concerto"*

Corelli's Concerto Grosso in G minor, Opus. 6, no. 8 (c. 1700), is inscribed *"Fatto per la notte di Natale,"* i.e. written for Christmas night, and includes a movement that imitates the *zampogna* or Italian shepherds' bagpipe, a characteristic instrument of the Christmas season in Rome.

"in the early days of classical music"

In saying this, Tom Sullivan ignores about 700 years of Medieval, Renaissance, and early Baroque music that preceded Corelli.

167. *"the vast Rubens with its dark–browed Jupiter"*

The painting, about 8 feet by 6, is *Cupid Supplicating Jupiter* by Peter Paul Rubens (1577–1640).

"the unfinished Death of Socrates"

This painting is attributed to the studio of Jacques–Louis David (1748–1825). Both paintings are in the Princeton Art Museum.

183. *"Gil would bungle...I would butcher"*

For *Take the 'A' Train,* see Authors' Note, *ROF,* p. 369. *La Follia* is the theme of a flashy set of variations that concludes Corelli's

Violin Sonata in D minor, Opus 5, no. 12.

185. "Bartholomew Cubbins or an illustrated Sherlock Holmes"

Reference is to *The Five Hundred Hats of Bartholomew Cubbins* (1938), an early work of Theodor Seuss Geisel (1904-1991), better known as Dr. Seuss.

189. "It is the greatest houses and the tallest trees"

Quoted from Herodotus, *The Histories,* 7.10e.

192. "Like Della and James in the O. Henry story"

The story in question is *The Gift of the Magi* by William Sydney Porter (1862-1910), who wrote novels as "O. Henry."

198. "An Edward Hopper painting of a woman"

Reference is to the painting *Morning Sun* (1952) by Edward Hopper (1882-1967), which is in the Columbus Museum of Art.

200. "Leonardo, in a letter to the Duke of Milan"

The Codex Atlanticus of Leonardo's writings contains the text of such a letter, written in 1482 or 83 (Richter no. 1340). It is one of the very few pieces written in the normal manner, rather than in Leonardo's customary mirror-writing, hence has been challenged as not genuine.

202. "The inhabitants of Utopia have two games"

From Book II of the *Utopia* of Thomas More (1478-1535), *Vol. 4, p. 129 of the Yale edition.*

204-205. "Eratosthenes approximated the earth's circumference" The Greek astronomer Eratosthenes of Cyrene (c. 276-c.194 BC) arrived at a figure of 252,000 stades. Opinions as to his margin of error from the current figure for the equatorial circumference (40,075 km) vary from 0.5 to 17%, depending on the size of the stade he used.

207. "number patterns containing arithmetical, geometric, or musical harmonies"

Such "harmonies," better known as "means," are three different ways of inserting a number m between two given numbers a and b. The arithmetical mean between 3 and 9 is 6 (formula: m =

a+b/2). The geometric mean between 4 and 9 is 6 (formula: a: m = m:b). The harmonic or musical mean between 3 and 6 is 4 (formula: m = 2ab/a+b).

209. "what Valla did with the Donation of Constantine"

Lorenzo Valla (1407–1457), using the newly-developed classical scholarship, proved in 1440 that the document known as the Donation of Constantine was a forgery. According to the document, the Emperor Constantine bequeathed his entire empire to the Roman Catholic Church. It was the basis for the Church's claim to exercise temporal as well as spiritual power; to dispute it counted as heresy as late as 1533. Valla realized that it was written in the debased Latin of several centuries after Constantine's time.

211. "Alberti wrote in the treatise I found"

The treatise is Alberti's *Della Pittura* (1435), and the quotation occurs towards the end of Book I.

212. "the names of those learned men whose wisdom forged my riddles"

On Pomponio Leto, see Chapter 4, On Lorenzo Valla, see note to p. 209. Jacques Lefèvre d'Étaples (1455–1537) studied at the Platonic Academy in Florence and became the primary French representative of the new Hermetic and Neoplatonic learning, first revealed in the Latin translations of Marsilio Ficino. On Alberti, see Chapter 3. On Alpago and Ibn al-Nafis, see notes to p. 239.

219. "Katie first saw the spot in a Walter Matthau movie"

See the Authors' Note, *ROF,* p. 370.

224. "There's more to 'love conquers all' than just the Prioress's brooch"

The Prioress is one of the pilgrims making their way to Canterbury in Chaucer's *Canterbury Tales.* Her brooch is described thus: "of small coral aboute hire arm she bar/a peire of bedes, gauded al with grene,/And theron heng a brooch of gold ful sheene/On which ther was first write a crowned A,/ And after *Amor vincit omnia.*" (General Prologue, 158–162)

"Agostino Carracci made this engraving"

The engraving by Agostino Carracci (1557–1602), dated 1599,

is the only illustration in *The Rule of Four* besides those from the *Hypnerotomachia*. The title, *Omnia vincit Amor*, appears in a cloud; the phrase comes from Virgil's Tenth Eclogue. Such designs were intended to be pondered over and deciphered, like emblems, but Patrick Sullivan's hints at the meaning of this one only complicate it. The women may be anonymous nymphs, but the one on the right, with a moon-shaped device above her brow, is probably the chaste goddess Diana, protecting her nymph-companion from sexual assault. The panpipes dropped on the ground show that the satyr is the god Pan, who is often shown at odds with Cupid/Amor. The victory of the infant god suggests the courtly sentiment that love conquers lust. However, Carracci also produced a drawing of the same subject in which Pan is getting the better of Amor, thrusting him away with a hand in his face. In the drawing, two other satyrs, one of them holding a rope, are lurking behind the tree. The nymphs are looking more distraught than in the engraving, for it seems that lust is going to overcome love. On many other aspects of this engraving and associated drawings and paintings, see Raichel Williamson, "*Omnia vincit Amor:* Un dipinto di Agostino Carracci," *Accademia Clementina, Atti e memorie,* new series 30-31 [1992], pp. 111-150.

225. *"I'm not sure how Chaucer's Prioress interpreted Virgil"*
Since she was a nun, she should have interpreted him as referring to sacred, rather than profane love.

226-27. *"An Italian professor named Ulisse Aldrovandi"*
Perhaps Tom Sullivan's study of Dr. Frankenstein's creation has led him to Aldrovandi (1522-1605), Bolognese physician, zoologist, and authority on monsters. Aldrovandi's *Ornithologia,* edition of Bologna, 1645, treats chickens ("De Gallo Gallinaceo") in Vol. II, xiv, pp. 183-352. Although Tom Sullivan exaggerates slightly, Aldrovandi does include chicken-related Augury, Prophecy, Dreams, Morals, Hieroglyphs, Emblems, Problems, Riddles, Medical use, Cooking, and Coins.

227. "Meanwhile Pliny the Elder…placed unicorns, basilisks, and manticores"

This is the case in Pliny's *Natural History*, Book VIII. See chapters xxix, 71 (rhinoceros), xxx, 75 (manticore), xxxi, 76 (unicorn), xxxiii, 78 (basilisk), and xxxiv, 80 (wolf). Pliny devotes many chapters to dolphins (IX, xix–xxxiii), especially mentioning their love of music. In Book X, lxxvi, 154–155, Pliny writes of how Julia Augusta, while pregnant with the future emperor Tiberius, carried an egg under her garments to ensure (not merely foretell) that the infant would be male.

229. "Horned beetles are hung around the necks of infants"

Pliny says this twice: in *Nat. Hist.,* XI, xxxiv, 97 and XXX, xlvii, 138. Compare the Mediterranean practice of hanging a horn-shaped coral around the neck, as protection against the Evil Eye.

"Cantharolethus"

Properly Cantharolethrus, which means "beetle-bane." *Nat. Hist.,* XI, xxxiv, 99.

230. "Aristotle says that insects don't inhale"

Cited in Pliny, *Nat. Hist.,* XI, cxii, 266. Aristotle comments on animals' memory in the *Parva Naturalia,* essay "On Memory," 450a.

236. "The night-owl, according to Horapollo"

See *Hieroglyphica* II, 25 for Horapollo's interpretation of what the Egyptians meant by their hieroglyphic of the night-owl, II, 41 for the beetle, and II, 96 for the eagle.

237. "the tower in the plain of Shinar"

Better known as the Tower of Babel; see Genesis 11:1–9. Note that the anger of the fictitious Colonna extends to the Old Testament God himself, consistently with the pagan nature of the *Hypnerotomachia*.

"Augustine, in contra Manichaeos"

Saint Augustine of Hippo (354–430) wrote several polemics against the followers of Mani. He treats the soul-body duality especially in *Concerning Two Souls, against the Manichaeans*.

"Descartes thought he could pinpoint the soul"
René Descartes (1596-1650) wrote on the pineal gland in his
Treatise on Man (1629-33), and at greater length in *The Passions of
the Soul* (1649).

238. *"Galen thought this is where vital spirits turned into animal ones"*
Galen of Pergamum (129-c.199) wrote on the *rete mirabile* in his
treatise *De Usu Partium* (On the use of the parts of the human
body). In animal anatomy it is called the retiform plexus. Galen,
finding it in sheep, mistakenly assumed that it existed in the human
body, too.

"Galen got it all wrong. He said there were little holes"
Galen states this in *On the Natural Faculties,* III, xv, 208.

239. *"Mondino made the same mistake"*
Mondino dei Luzzi (c. 1270-c. 1326) wrote the standard
handbook of dissection, slavishly following Galen's authority
rather than experimental evidence.

"Vesalius and Servetus figured it out"
The *Fabrica* (1543) of Andreas Vesalius (1514-1564) was the
first modern treatise on anatomical dissection, and, like the
Hypnerotomachia, a prized example of early book illustration.
Michael Servetus (1511-1553) privately published his discovery
in a theological treatise. For the heresies contained therein, he was
burned at the stake by order of the Reformer John Calvin.

"Harvey didn't discover the circulatory system until the 1600s"
William Harvey (1578-1657) published his discovery in 1628.

"The Arabs figured it out two hundred years before"
The Arab physician Ibn al-Nafis (1210/11-1288) found that
the wall between the ventricles of the heart was solid, disputed
Galen, and was the first to describe the pulmonary circulation of
the blood.

"Francesco must've gotten the text from Andrea Alpago"
Sixteenth century editor of Avicenna and other Arabic writers.

270. *"Aldus Manutius, took his famous dolphin and anchor emblem"*

See illustrations 21-22. The dolphin was believed in ancient times to be the fastest fish in the sea, and its coupling with the anchor typified the motto *Festina lente*, "Hasten slowly." This is a principle Poliphilo constantly has to keep in mind, as his impulses tend to run away with him. It is also good advice for a printing-shop, or any business in which excessive haste only ends up costing more time.

278. "In every other discipline, you've got the biggest names in Europe"

As the Authors' Note remarks (*ROF* p. 369), these names are not all of contemporaries, but they serve to convey the importance of Florentine culture for two and a half centuries, from the time of Dante to that of Michelangelo.

279. "A Dominican monk was sent to Florence"

On Savonarola, see Chapter 4.

"Prospero Colonna, Francesco's uncle, allegedly dies of gout"

On the suspicious deaths of a number of eminent people in the last years of the fifteenth century, see Chapter 4.

280. "the Cupid figure was supposed to be Piero, the new Medici heir"

When Lorenzo the Magnificent died in 1492, his son Piero took over the Medici role as democratic dictators of Florence. Piero (1472-1503) was nicknamed "il Sfortunato" (the Unfortunate) or "il Fatuo" (the Fatuous). When the French attacked the city, he panicked and surrendered, for which the Florentines expelled him and his family in 1494. (See Chapter 4) The interpretation of the illustration and story in the *Hypnerotomachia* as referring to Piero is an ingenious invention.

285. "Works that no one has seen for hundreds of years"

These are all genuinely lost works, known to have existed from their mention in classical literature. Colonna's searches and discoveries resemble the actual retrieval of classical work from remote corners of Europe and the Mediterranean, as it took place throughout the fifteenth century. There is one exception: a large portion of the Greek poem called *The Chaldaean Oracles* was preserved by Neoplatonic authors, and served in the Renaissance as witness to the teachings of Zoroaster.

287. "One was Terragni, the architect"

The character of Terragni, who is given no other name, appears
to be fictitious.

290. "He delivers a line from the Gospel of Paul"

This is a surprising mistake for Paul Harris to have made,
especially after his parochial orphanage education. Saint Paul
wrote no Gospel, only Epistles. These lines are paraphrased from
the First Epistle to the Corinthians 1:26-28 and 3:18-20.

293. "Inde ferunt, totidem qui vivere debeat annos"

The myth of the phoenix is told in Ovid, *Metamorphoses,* XV,
393-406. After five hundred years, it builds a pyre of aromatic
woods and burns itself to death, whereupon a new phoenix arises
from the ashes. Its rebirth is neatly reflected in the length of time
between the publication of the *Hypnerotomachia* (1499) and the
rediscovery of Colonna's secret, as told in the novel, in 1999.

364. "an Eakins painting of a lone rower on the Schuylkill River"

The Philadelphia painter Thomas Eakins (1844-1916) specialized
in rowing scenes. The reference may be to his painting *Max Schmitt
in a Single Scull* (1871), now in the Metropolitan Museum of Art,
New York.

365. "On the bases of the statuary had been painted three inscriptions"

The two following quotations are from Genesis 41:56 and 43:30.

366. "'little barrel,' or Botticelli"

Sandro Botticelli (1445-1510) painted many sacred scenes,
including large-scale frescoes in the Sistine Chapel, and several
notable pagan subjects including *The Birth of Venus, The Primavera,*
and *Pallas and the Centaur.* No painting by him of Joseph or of
an Egyptian setting is known to exist. Anecdotal evidence has
been inflated to make Botticelli seem a convert to Savonarola's
principles, and efforts have been made to interpret his later
paintings in this light. Stanley Meltzoff (see Bibliography) shows
that the contrary is the case. Botticelli's enigmatic painting *The
Calumny of Apelles* was intended as a work of symbolic instruction

to the young Piero de' Medici, urging him not to listen to the anti-
humanist factions. It was a defense of the freedom of poets and
painters to use classical inspiration and pagan subjects, as against
Savonarola and other enemies of classical learning.

Bibliography

Calvesi, Maurizio, *La "Pugna d'amore in sogno" di Francesco Colonna Romano,* Rome: Lithos Editrice, 1996.

Casella, Maria Theresa and Giovanni Pozzi, *Francesco Colonna. Biografia e opere,* 2 vols., Padua: Editrice Antenore, 1959. [C&P]

The Chemical Wedding of Christian Rosenkreutz, translated by Joscelyn Godwin, Grand Rapids: Phanes Press, 1991.

Colonna, Francesco, *Hypnerotomachia Poliphili,* edited with commentary by Giovanni Pozzi and Lucia A. Ciapponi, 2 vols., Padua: Editrice Antenore, 1980. [P&C]

Colonna, Francesco, *Hypnerotomachia Poliphili,* facsimile, translated and edited with commentaries by Marco Ariani and Mino Gabriele, 2 vols., Milan: Adelphi Edizioni, 1998. [A&G]

Colonna, Francesco, *Hypnerotomachia Poliphili: The Strife of Love in a Dream,* translated, with an introduction, by Joscelyn Godwin, London and New York: Thames & Hudson, 1999. [HP]

Colonna, Francesco, *Le Songe de Poliphile,* Paris: Kerver, 1546. [*Songe*]

The Fame and Confession of the Fraternity of R: C: Commonly of the Rosie Cross, facsimile of London, 1652 edition, Margate: Societas Rosicruciana in Anglia, 1923.

Fierz-David, Linda, *The Dream of Poliphilo: The Soul in Love,* translated by Mary Hottinger, Dallas: Spring Publications, 1987.

Godwin, Joscelyn, *The Pagan Dream of the Renaissance,* Grand Rapids: Phanes Press; London: Thames & Hudson, 2003.

Godwin, Joscelyn, "Poliphilo's Dream, or Alberti's?" [review of Liane Lefaivre's *Leon Battista Alberti's Hypnerotomachia Poliphili*] in *Design Book Review,* 41/42 (2000), pp. 48-52.

Kretzulesco-Quaranta, Emanuela, *Les jardins du songe: "Poliphile" et la mystique de la Renaissance,* Paris: Les Belles Lettres, 1976, second revised edition 1986. [*Jardins*]

Kretzulesco, Nicola & Emanuela, *Giardini misterici: Misteri, Simboli, Enigmi, dall'Antichità al Novecento,* Parma: Silva Editore, 1994. [*Giardini*]

Lefaivre, Liane, *Leon Battista Alberti's Hypnerotomachia Poliphili: Re-Cognizing the Architectural Body in the Early Italian Renaissance,* Cambridge, Mass.: MIT Press, 1997.

Leitch, Alexander, *A Princeton Companion,* Princeton: Princeton University Press, 1978.

Lunn, Martin, *Da Vinci Code Decoded,* New York:
Disinformation Company, 2004.

Palermino, Richard J., "The Roman Academy, the Catacombs
and the Conspiracy of 1468," *Archivium historiae pontificae* 18
(1980), pp. 117-155.

Mallinger, Jean, "Storia segreta dell'ordine pitagorico II°,"
Politica Romana 2 (1995), pp. 109-119.

Meltzoff, Stanley, *Botticelli, Signorelli and Savonarola.* Theologia
Poetica *and Painting from Boccaccio to Poliziano,* Florence: Leo S.
Olschki, 1987.

Ragon, J.M., "Storia segreta dell'ordine pitagorico," *Politica
Romana* 1 (1994), pp. 69-81.

Steinberg, Ronald M., *Fra Girolamo Savonarola, Florentine Art, and
Renaissance Historiography,* Athens: Ohio University Press, 1977.

Index to *The Rule of Four*

(Page references are to the first U.S. edition)

Index to The Real Rule of Four